Illustrator
Howard Chaney

Editor
Marsha Kearns

Editorial Project Manager
Ina Massler Levin, M.A.

Editor-in-Chief
Sharon Coan, M.S. Ed.

Art Director
Elayne Roberts

Associate Designer
Denise Bauer

Cover Artist
Larry Bauer

Product Manager
Phil Garcia

Imaging
James Edward Grace

Publishers
Rachelle Cracchiolo, M.S. Ed.
Mary Dupuy Smith, M.S. Ed.

Author

Michelle Breyer, M.A.

Teacher Created Materials, Inc.
6421 Industry Way
Westminster, CA 92683
www.teachercreated.com

©1998 Teacher Created Materials, Inc.
Reprinted, 2000
Made in U.S.A.
ISBN-1-57690-215-3

TABLE OF CONTENTS

INTRODUCTION

The *Brain Teasers* series provides fun ways to exercise and develop brain power! Each page stands alone and can be used as a quick and easy filler activity. The pages can be distributed to students as individual worksheets or made into transparencies for presentation to the entire class at once. The activities are especially useful in helping students develop:

- Logic and other critical thinking skills.
- Creative thinking skills.
- Research skills.
- Spelling skills.

- General vocabulary skills.
- General knowledge skills.
- Spatial skills.

This world history activity book pays particular attention to the ancient civilizations that shaped our young world. Use the activities with your social studies curriculum to introduce and reinforce learning—or just for fun! Every effort was made to ensure this book presents the most accurate and current data available.

GEOGRAPHY JEOPARDY

Use the geographic features in the box below to form appropriate questions for the given answers.

1. The lush region that formed a great arc from the eastern shore of the Mediterranean Sea to the Persian Gulf.

   What is the_____?

2. The waterway that extends north of the Dead Sea.

   What is the _____?

3. A small island off the coast of Syria in the Mediterranean Sea.

   What is _____?

4. The northernmost waterway that bounded the Mesopotamia region.

   What is the _____?

5. The capital of the ancient Hittite Empire in Asia Minor.

   What is _____?

6. The body of water that separates the Sinai Peninsula from Africa.

   What is the _____?

7. The place where Moses wrote the Ten Commandments.

   What is _____?

8. The ancient capital for King Nebuchadnezzar, who built the famous hanging gardens.

   What is _____?

9. The largest body of water in the ancient world.

   What is the _____?

10. The huge expanse of barren land on the Sinai Peninsula, across which Moses led his exodus.

    What is the _____?

11. A body of water near Jerusalem where the ancient scrolls of the Bible were found.

    What is the _____?

12. Now known as Iraq, the land believed to be the cradle of civilization.

    What is _____?

Geographical Features

Euphrates River	Mediterranean	Mount Sinai	Hattusa	Nile River
Jordan River	Sea	Cyprus	Mesopotamia	Jerusalem
Fertile Crescent	Red Sea	Arabian Desert	Babylon	Syrian Desert
Tigris River	Dead Sea			

SUMERIAN INVENTIONS

Unscramble the words to discover some inventions developed by the Ancient Sumerians. Add other inventions to each category.

Transportation

1. elehwed hicleves_____

2. bastosila_____

   other:_____

Farming

3. agiritonir mestyss_____

4. sedik_____

5. naclas_____

   other:_____

Crafts

6. epocrp stolo_____

7. zebrno ewapsno_____

8. lyrewje_____

9. toreypt hewle_____

10. ickbrs_____

    other:_____

Education

11. ecuminrof girnwit_____

12. ologymyth_____

    other:_____

Mathematics

13. lendacar_____

14. colck nitemus_____

15. sniut fo sumanerteme_____

    other:_____

CONTRIBUTIONS AND ACHIEVEMENTS

Match the civilization with its contribution and/or achievement.

Sumerians	Hebrews
Assyrians	Hittites
Babylonians	Phoenicians

_____ 1. Created the first written public laws, Hammurabi's code, which described rules and consequences for social behavior

_____ 2. Created the first civilization by establishing an agricultural community in the Mesopotamia region

_____ 3. Experts in trade and sailing who created travel logs and maps of the ancient world

_____ 4. Created the first peace treaty

_____ 5. Developed advanced weapons and strategies, which they used to conquer the ancient world

_____ 6. First to develop iron weapons

_____ 7. Built the Hanging Gardens and a magnificent ziggurat

_____ 8. Developed cuneiform, the earliest form of writing

_____ 9. First to believe in and spread the concept of one God

_____ 10. Developed the first irrigation systems, with dikes and canals

_____ 11. Developed the 60-minute hour to conform to the base-60 math system of the Sumerians

_____ 12. Wrote the Torah and the Old Testament, the first half of the Bible

_____ 13. Developed the first alphabet

_____ 14. Created the first wheeled vehicles for transporting goods and people

WHAT'S IN A NAME?

Unscramble the following names from the age of the ancient Isralites. Then write each name in the appropriate box.

1. olsonom   _____

2. astolez   _____

3. vidad   _____

4. eoding   _____

5. dujas   _____

6. escacabem   _____

7. seoms   _____

8. masnos   _____

9. thailgo   _____

10. usal   _____

11. susje   _____

12. drohe   _____

13. thesre   _____

14. nadeil   _____

15. shojau   _____

16. thru   _____

17. hamarab   _____

18. ahon   _____

19. stiplihines   _____

20. marsaitnas   _____

21. yrma   _____

22. lilahde   _____

23. haresesip   _____

24. leisestria   _____

Men

Women

Groups

COMPARE LAWS

The Babylonians and the Hebrews both instituted rules for law and order in the ancient world. Read the descriptions below, and write the letter in the correct box.

Hammurabi's Code	Hebrew Law

A. The Ten Commandments were presented to the people by Moses

B. The 282 laws describing the rules and consequences for society's behavior

C. Laws organized into categories such as business, family, marriage, farming, etc.

D. More humane than other laws of the time. The rules of conduct discussed charity to others, freeing slaves, and not punishing children for their parent's crimes

E. Handed down by God to reflect God's will

F. Written by the king of Babylonia who ruled from 1728–1686 B.C.

G. Part of this law defined moral sins as opposed to laws and punishment

H. Carved into a huge stone pillar at the temple

I. Created the roots for Judaism, Christianity, and Islam

J. Carved into two stone tablets and presented to the people

K. Based on "an eye for an eye" principle, but punishments differed based on social class

L. Handed down by the sun god Shamash, who was also considered the god of justice

M. Author claimed that God called on him "to make justice visible in the land" and to "destroy the wicked person and evil doer so that the strong may not injure the weak"

On the back, compare and contrast the two systems of justice. Then describe how our laws today reflect both of these ancient sets of crime and punishment.

CRACK THE CODE

Babylonian numbers have been used to write an ancient proverb. Use the key to translate the Babylonian numbers into Arabic numbers. Then use the alphabet chart to change the Arabic numbers into letters and decode the proverb. The first letter has been done for you.

<<IIII **24** I	I<IIII IIII		I<<<III III	I<IIII IIII	
	<III II	I<<IIII <<	<II	I<IIII IIII	
<<<IIII <<	<III II	<<III <<	<<<IIII III	III III	
I<<<III III		I<<IIII	<<IIII III	I<<<III <<II	
<II	I<IIII IIII	<<<IIII III	<II	I<<II	I<III II

Babylonian Numbers

A thin wedge pointing down **I** means 1 or 60.

A fat wedge pointing left **<** means 10.

For example: 13 = **<III** (10+3)   34 = **<<<IIII** (10+10+10+4)

81 = **I<<I** (60+10+10+1)

Alphabet Chart

A=96	F=84	K=22	O=15	S=75	W=71
B=7	G=60	L=27	P=104	T=37	X=89
C=14	H=6	M=54	Q=44	U=43	Y=115
D=55	I=24	N=78	R=82	V=35	Z=109
E=12	J=95				

On the back, write what you think this proverb means.

DUOS AND TRIOS

Read the sets of words and decide how they go together. Then explain their connection and importance.

1. Tigris River and Euphrates River _____

_____

2. Ziggurat and the Hanging Gardens of Babylon _____

_____

3. Cuneiform writing, Babylonian numbers, and Phoenician alphabet_____

_____

4. Moses and Hammurabi _____

_____

5. Gilgamesh and Enkidu of Uruk _____

_____

6. Copper, bronze, and iron _____

_____

7. Wheeled vehicles and sailboats_____

_____

8. Tyre and Sidon _____

_____

9. Babylon, Nineveh, and Ur _____

_____

10. Caspian Sea, Persian Gulf, and Red Sea _____

_____

WHO'S WHO IN THE MIDDLE EAST?

Match each name to his description.

Moses	Hiram the Great	Hattusili II	King Gilgamesh
Ibbi-Sin	Hammurabi	Abraham	Antiochus
Nebuchadnezzar	Ashurbanipal	Sir Leonard Woolley	King David

_____ 1. This famous Sumerian king was recorded in the world's first epic tale with his friend and adviser Enkidu. He was king of the city of Uruk around 2700 B.C.

_____ 2. The last of the Assyrian kings, he lived in a lush palace near the Tigris River. He held lavish dinner parties and enjoyed hunting. He created the first library, which contained over 22,000 clay cuneiform tablets.

_____ 3. This leader of the ancient Israelites led his people on a 40-year exodus through the Arabian desert to escape persecution in Egypt.

_____ 4. He ruled Babylonia from 605–562 B.C. He built a large ziggurat and created the famous Hanging Gardens of Babylon. Although he was considered a good king by his people, the ancient Israelites did not like him because he sent them into exile.

_____ 5. This citizen of Ur formed a new tribe of people and took them to Canaan. They became the first documented evidence of the Hebrew civilization.

_____ 6. This Hittite king created the first peace treaty with King Ramses II of Egypt around 1284 B.C. for protection against the Assyrians.

_____ 7. He was king of the Israelites around 1000 B.C. and made Jerusalem the capital of the kingdom. He was concerned with trying to solve many social problems.

_____ 8. This Babylonian king ruled from around 1728–1686 B.C. He wrote the first laws that governed a kingdom. His code addressed many of the same problems people have had throughout the ages.

_____ 9. He was the last king of Ur around 2000 B.C. He held off the attack by desert tribesmen but was sent no help by other Sumerian city-states. He was taken away as a prisoner while the city and its great temple were destroyed.

_____10. This ruler from Syria around 200 B.C. forced Greek culture and religion on the Jews. Chanukah is the celebration of the miracle of the Jewish revolt against his practices.

_____11. He discovered the city of Ur in 1927 on an archeological dig in Iraq. He uncovered a vast burial ground that revealed the lost civilization of Sumer.

_____12. This great ruler of Tyre set up trade routes throughout the Mediterranean and helped make Phoenicia the home of expert sailors.

EGYPTIAN SYMBOLS

Match the pictures with their descriptions.

_____ 1. A symbol for everlasting life, often worn as an amulet on the wrist or ankle.

_____ 2. The symbol for the royalty that ruled a particular region in Egypt, often worn on the headdress of the pharaoh.

_____ 3. The symbol for the union of upper and lower Egypt into one land, first used by King Menes.

_____ 4. These symbolic figures, called shabtis, represent the workers in the afterlife that would till the soil in the Field of Reeds for the dead pharaoh.

_____ 5. The symbol for protection and mysticism, said to come from Horus.

_____ 6. The symbols for leadership and royalty, seen in the hands of Osiris and often pictured in the hands of the pharaohs.

_____ 7. This symbol represented King Akhenaten's belief in one god called Aten.

_____ 8. A symbol of the pharaoh, Queen Hatshepsut also wore one.

_____ 9. A symbol believed to have magical powers for healing and mysticism today.

_____10. The symbol for judgment, used to determine whether or not a soul is noble and pure enough to enter an afterlife in the Field of Reeds. Today the symbol represents justice.

_____11. The sacred symbol for Amon-Re, the sun god, who carried his daily ball of fire across the sky. It was often used as an amulet or a personal seal and represented everlasting life.

_____12. The symbol for a particular region in Egypt and a great dynasty, often seen drawn on the chest of a mummy.

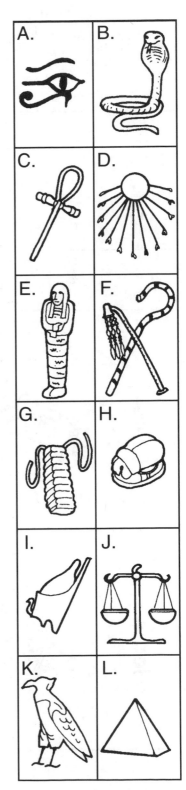

CONCENTRATION

Make a deck of 30 cards by cutting apart the pictures and descriptions of important Egyptian gods on pages 12–15. Shuffle the cards and lay them facedown in a grid. With a partner, play Concentration by turning over two cards at a time to make a match of the picture and description. The player with the most matches wins.

Aten

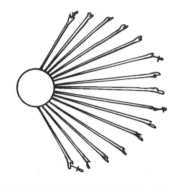

He is another form of the sun god. He is unlike any of the other gods, neither human nor animal. This sun disc with outstretched arms holds an ankh, representing everlasting life. He is the one and only god worshipped during the reign of King Akhenaten.

Osiris

He presides over the Underworld, where he is the judge of the dead. A son of Nut and Geb, he married his sister, Isis, with whom he had a son, Horus. He represents immortality and is depicted as a mummy in a royal crown holding the crook and flail, the signs of sovereignty and power. Sometimes he is white (mummy wrappings), sometimes black (the Underworld), and sometimes green (spring and resurrection).

Horus

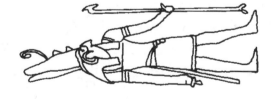

He leads the dead to the Underworld to be judged by the weighing of their hearts. He is the son of Isis and Osiris. In mythology, he avenged the death of his father by killing Seth. During the battle he lost an eye, which was renewed by Isis. You see the Eye of Horus in paintings, amulets, and jewelry, representing renewal and protection. He is sometimes depicted as the head of a falcon or as an entire falcon wearing a crown.

CONCENTRATION *(cont.)*

Isis

She is goddess of magic and healing and the sister and wife to Osiris. She wears a headdress shaped like a seat. Some believe it is her tears for her dead husband that flood the Nile each year.

Seth

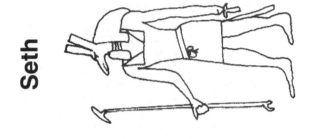

Lord of the desert he is also the god of storms, violence, and disorder. He is the evil brother of Osiris and therefore another son of Nut and Geb. His battle with Horus illustrates the battle of night with day and the contest between good and evil. He is represented with the head of an unidentified animal.

Thoth

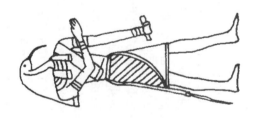

God of wisdom and science, he is the scribe of the god world, recording all writing, counting, and measurement. Since he records time, he is also the god of the moon. He is husband to Ma'at and represented by the head of an ibis. Many times he is holding tools for writing or measuring.

Anubis

God of embalming, he presides over the mummification process. He is messenger to Osiris and guard of the scales during the weighing of the heart ceremony. Priests wear his jackal head during rituals performed when working on a mummy.

CONCENTRATION *(cont.)*

Ptah

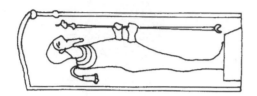

He is the parson of craftsmen, since it is believed that he invented the arts. He is the local god of Memphis, one of the ancient capitals of Egypt, and husband to Sekhmet. He is shown as a hairless, mummy-like figure holding a large tool, and at the opening of the mouth ceremony during mummification, he uses the tool he holds.

H'apy

He is the god of the Nile and responsible for the proper workings of this precious river. He is usually shown as a long-haired man with papyrus and lotus flowers growing from the top of his head. He also has the chest of a woman, depicting fertility. He lives in a cave at the head of the Nile.

Nut

She is the goddess of the sky and heavens. She is sister and wife to Geb and mother of Osiris and Seth. She is believed to be one of the first gods. Usually she is represented as a lady arching over the earth god, Geb. Sometimes she is seen as a large cow, and sometimes she is depicted with stars, representing the night sky.

Ma'at

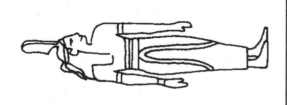

She is the goddess of law and order, truth, and balance. The Egyptians required precise order in their daily lives; they believed that without this balance and harmony, the world would be filled with destruction and chaos. She is the daughter of Re and wife of Thoth. The ostrich feather she wears on her head is put on the scales during the judgment ceremony. Sometimes she is shown sitting on the tip of the scales, and sometimes her entire body is being weighed on the scales itself.

14

CONCENTRATION *(cont.)*

Bastet

She is the household goddess representing joy and music. She is depicted as a cat—an animal prized in Ancient Egypt to keep rodents under control.

Geb

He is the god of the earth. He usually poses below his sister/wife, Nut. Sometimes he is shown with a goose on his head, representing one of the many creation myths in which he laid the egg from which the world sprang.

Sekhmet

She is the goddess of war and consulted by pharaohs. She brings destruction to all enemies of Re. It was believed that her fiery breath was the hot winds of the Egyptian desert. She is wife to Ptah and has the head of a lion.

Hathor

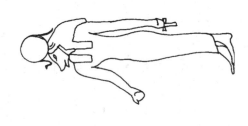

She is goddess of love, beauty, dancing, and music and protector of children and birth. She is often shown as a beautiful woman with the sun disc and horns of a cow. Sometimes she is depicted as a cow with the sun disc between her horns.

IT'S IN THE NAME

Write the name of the Egyptian ruler whose name contains the following word:

1. ram_____

2. pat_____

3. hen_____

4. tank_____

Write the name of the ruler whose name fits these humorous clues:

5. Her name sounds like a line of clothing fit for a queen._____

6. His name sounds like a sneeze._____

7. His name sounds like snoring._____

8. His name sounds like a brand of sleeping pill for sheep._____

9. His name inspires the "utmost" respect._____

Write the name of the ruler each numbered item describes.

10._____ She had love affairs with Julius Caesar and Mark Antony. She tried to keep Egypt as a major world power but failed and committed suicide.

11._____ She was the first woman to rule Egypt as a pharaoh. She ruled for over 20 years and proved to be a skillful leader. She expanded trade for Egypt and built a great obelisk at the temple to Amon-Re. She supported domestic projects that restored Egypt's beauty.

12._____ He unified Upper and Lower Egypt.

13._____ He began the age of pyramid building by creating the step pyramid around 2650 B.C.

14._____ He is credited with building the pyramids in Giza that were the largest ever built. His son eventually built the Sphinx.

15._____ He believed in one god, named Aten, and attempted to convert his people. He changed the rules for art by allowing artists to paint and carve as they truly saw the world rather than by using predetermined mathematical formulas. He was married to the famed beauty Nefertiti.

16._____ Although he reigned for only a short time, he is perhaps the most famous of all pharaohs. His tomb was discovered by Howard Carter, and the treasures found within have toured the world.

WHAT IS IT?

Cut out the squares and put them back together to form the image of a famous Egyptian work of art.

PYRAMID PUZZLE

Fill in the blanks within the statements about pyramid building. Once complete, match the letters to answer the riddle at the bottom of the page.

1. Select the proper __ __ __ __ to build the pyramid.
   4 2 7 19

2. Clear the __ __ __ __ __ __ __ __ __ __ of loose sand, gravel, and rock.
   9 1 11 16 13 8 7 2 1 16

3. Using astronomy and __ __ __ __ __ __ __ __ find true north to
   14 19 1 17 19 7 10 12
   ensure that the pyramid walls face north, south, east and __ __ __ __.
   6 19 4 7

4. Make sure the site is __ __ __ __ __ by digging channels and filling them with
   20 19 15 19 20
   __ __ __ __ __.
   6 8 7 19 10

5. Mark the water level and clear excess __ __ __ __.
   13 2 10 7

6. Use geometry to make sure the leveled __ __ __ __ is perfectly square.
   3 8 4 19

7. Measure, cut, and move the __ __ __ __ __ __ __ __ __ slabs onto
   20 2 17 19 4 7 1 16 19
   boats, using __ __ __ __ as rollers.
   20 1 14 4

8. Transport the limestone slabs across the __ __ __ __ River to the building site.
   16 2 20 19

9. Once at the building site, transport the limestone slabs onto __ __ __ __ __
   4 20 19 13 4
   and up ramps to their positions on the pyramid.

10. Place the __ __ __ __ __ __ __ __ atop the completed pyramid.
    18 8 21 4 7 1 16 19

11. Starting at the __ __ __, smooth and __ __ __ __ __ __ the sides,
    7 1 21   21 1 20 2 4 5
    removing the dirt ramps as you work to the __ __ __ __.
    3 8 4 19

Why did the pharaohs of Egypt build pyramids?

__ __   __ __ __ __   __
7 1   5 8 15 19   8

__ __ __ __ __ __ __ __   __ __
4 7 8 2 10 6 8 12   7 1

__ __ __ __ __ __
5 19 8 15 19 16

BOOK OF THE DEAD

The Book of the Dead was a collection of verses, prayers, hymns, and petitions to help the deceased on their journey into the afterlife. Use the key to translate the petition below.   First change the Egyptian numbers into the Arabic numbers we use today. Then use the alphabet code to translate the Arabic numbers into letters.

_____ | 9 ___ my _____ ||||∩∩ _____ ∩ ∩ ∩ _____ |∩999 _____ ||∩ _____ ||∩∩∩ ,

_____ |∩∩ _____ | 9 _____ not _____ ||||| _____ ||∩∩∩ _____ |∩999 _____ |||∩ _____ |∩∩ ___ as

witness _____ |∩999 _____ |∩∩∩ _____ |∩999 _____ |9999 _____ |||∩ _____ ||||| _____ ||∩∩∩

me! Do _____ |||∩ _____ | 9 _____ ||∩∩∩ ___ oppose _____ ∩∩∩9 _____ ∩ ∩ ∩ ___ in

_____ ||∩∩∩ _____ ||||∩∩ _____ ∩ ∩ ∩ ___ judgment. Do not _____ ||∩∩9 _____ ∩ ∩ ∩ ___ hostile

_____ ||∩∩∩ _____ | 9 _____ ∩∩∩9 _____ ∩ ∩ ∩ ___ in the presence _____ | 9 _____ ∩99 ___ the

_____ ||∩∩ _____ ∩ ∩ ∩ _____ ∩ ∩ ∩ _____ ∩ _____ ∩ ∩ ∩ _____ ||∩ ___ of the

_____ |||∩∩9 _____ |∩999 _____ 9 _____ |∩999 _____ |||∩ _____ ∩∩∩∩ _____ ∩ ∩ ∩ .

Egyptian Numbers

1 = a staff | 10 = an arch ∩   100 = a coiled rope 9

A particular number is written by writing the number of ones, then tens, then hundreds.

Example: 13= |||∩   72= ||∩∩∩∩∩∩∩   321= |∩∩999

Alphabet Code

A = 311	F = 210	K = 22	O = 101	S = 5	W = 62
B = 123	G = 31	L = 100	P = 10	T = 32	X = 39
C = 40	H = 24	M = 130	Q = 48	U = 380	Y = 6
D = 21	I = 401	N = 13	R = 12	V = 45	Z = 125
E = 30	J = 72				

Why would the deceased use this petition with Anubis?

RHYME TIME

Answer the riddles by writing a word that rhymes with the clue in the word box.

1. The Egyptians took this out through the nostrils._____

2. A completed one was wrapped in yards of linen._____

3. It was considered the center of knowledge and emotion. _____

4. Linens were scented with these. _____

5. This was made in the abdomen. _____

6. When empty, it was filled with rags. _____

7. Eye sockets looked black because of this. _____

8. Its job was to drain the body of moisture. _____

9. He wore a mask of Anubis while working. _____

10. A sarcophogus goes in this. _____

11. This is woven to make linen. _____

12. King Tut's is famous. _____

train	dozen
dummy	patron
start	yeast
boils and rice	zoom
decision	stacks
best	task

Unscramble these related words.

13. camuimifimont_____

14. piconac rajs_____

15. malp newi _____

16. nemabod_____

17. lanirent gornas _____

18. pocarshosug _____

19. To what subject in Egyptian history do all of these words relate? _____

_____

TEST YOUR FASHION SENSE

Below are some silly statements made about Egyptian fashion. Substitute a word from the box for each underlined word to make the statements true.

1. Women wore long dresses called <u>tubes</u>. Those of wealthy women were <u>torn</u> and woven with threads of <u>horsehair</u>.

2. Men wore linen kilts called <u>bumbleshoots</u> that were wrapped around their <u>fingers</u> and secured with elaborate <u>staples</u>.

3. Men and women wore <u>daisies</u> on their feet. They were made of <u>mashed potatoes</u> or leather and secured with a <u>feather</u> between the toes.

4. The wealthy wore headdresses or <u>pigs</u> made from real hair and <u>elephant</u> fibers. Common Egyptians wore <u>plastic</u> headdresses or headbands.

5. Scented <u>puddings</u> and creams were applied to protect the <u>cactus</u> from the hot desert climate.

6. Women <u>licked</u> their eyebrows and <u>danced</u> them in an exaggerated shape with black <u>licorice</u>.

7. Men and women also used kohl to paint <u>circles</u> around their eyes to reduce the sun's <u>laughter</u>.

8. Cheeks and lips were colored red, using <u>chili peppers</u> mixed with <u>soda pop</u>.

9. On special occasions they used <u>spaghetti</u> to decorate their fingernails, palms, <u>lizards</u>, and the soles of their <u>shoes</u>.

10. Collars of gold and precious <u>marbles</u> were fashionable. They were usually <u>glued</u> at the back of the <u>classroom</u>.

knots	wigs	gems
plucked	sandals	pleated
shentis	vegetable	ochre
toenails	sheaths	henna
waists	gold	animal fat
thong	skin	lines
neck	feet	cloth
kohl	glare	painted
oils	reed	tied

WHO IS IT?

Fill in the blanks to complete the five letter words. When read from top to bottom, the word made by the center letters will spell the name of a Greek god. The first one has been done for you.

1.

```
D A [Z] E D
F L [E] A S
F L [U] N K
B A [S] I S
```

2.

```
S T [ ] N D
B U [ ] N T
B R [ ] A D
B U [ ] E S
```

3.

```
A S [ ] E S
D R [ ] A M
P A [ ] T Y
G A [ ] E S
C L [ ] A N
W I [ ] E R
```

4.

```
O T [ ] E R
C H [ ] A T
C U [ ] L Y
S T [ ] M P
```

5.

```
P L [ ] N E
G U [ ] S Y
O T [ ] E R
S T [ ] A M
W I [ ] K S
B R [ ] I N
```

6.

```
A S [ ] E N
T R [ ] I N
F A [ ] E S
F L [ ] S H
L O [ ] E R
```

7.

```
A S [ ] E S
P L [ ] A T
D U [ ] T Y
E A [ ] E N
C L [ ] N G
S H [ ] M E
```

8.

```
P L [ ] T E
P A [ ] E R
F L [ ] A T
B U [ ] L Y
G U [ ] P S
C H [ ] R E
```

9.

```
H I [ ] E S
B L [ ] N D
D I [ ] E S
C L [ ] A R
B A [ ] H S
S T [ ] R N
F I [ ] E D
```

FAMOUS GREEKS

Circle the correct answer for each statement. Then fill in the code at the bottom with the correct letters to find this famous quote from the Greek statesman Pericles.

1. The famous poet Sappho was a male.   True=L   False=N
2. Socrates committed suicide.   True=E   False=B
3. The Theory of Displacement was discovered
   by Archimedes.   True=O   False=A
4. Thales was a philosopher who believed the gods
   made earthquakes.   True=S   False=I
5. Herodotus is called "the father of history."   True=U   False=Y
6. Pericles fought bravely in the Persian Wars and
   became the leader of Athens.   True=N   False=Q
7. Pythagoras discovered the formula for finding the
   hypotenuse of a triangle.   True=L   False=M
8. Doctors today take an oath written by Hippocrates.   True=R   False=E
9. Sophocles wrote the famous play *Antigone*.   True=V   False=H
10. Euclid is known as "the mother of geometry."   True=C   False=A
11. The Grecian telegraph was invented by
    Alexander the Great.   True=L   False=B
12. Plato was a philosophy student of Aristotle.   True=G   False=Y
13. Aristarchus discovered the Earth revolves
    around the sun.   True=F   False=D
14. The palace at Knossos was built by King Midas.   True=P   False=T
15. The Peloponnesian War was recorded by
    Thucydides.   True=W   False=C
16. Homer wrote the *Iliad* and *Odyssey* in
    the 500s B.C.   True=V   False=H
17. Darius was a Persian general who fought
    against the Athenians.   True=S   False=O

"__ __ __ __ __ __ __ __   __ __
  2   9   2   8   12 3   1   2   4   17

__ __ __ __ __   __ __ __ __ __ __
  2   6   5   10 7   11 2   13 3   8   2

__ __ __   __ __ __."
 14 16 2   7   10 15

WHICH IS IT?

Circle the correct response for each question regarding facts about ancient Greece.

1. Which is farther north—Thessaly or Attica?

2. Which is the bigger island—Crete or Rhodes?

3. Which lies west of Greece—the Ionian Sea or the Aegean Sea?

4. Which is farther south—Athens or Sparta?

5. Which came first—the Minoan Age or the Mycenaean Age?

6. Which work of literature by Homer came first—the *Iliad* or the *Odyssey*?

7. Which type of Athenian government came first—a monarchy or an oligarchy?

8. Which group of people made up the larger part of Athenian society—the male citizens or the slaves?

9. Which city contained the Temple of Apollo—Olympia or Delphi?

10. Which god was honored at the Olympics—Zeus or Apollo?

11. Which god was honored at the drama festivals—Athena or Dionysius?

12. Which happened first—the Persian Wars or the Peloponnesian Wars?

13. Which structure is dedicated to Athena—the Parthenon or the Agora?

14. Which famous Greek died first— Socrates or Pericles?

15. Which ruler reigned during the Hellenistic Age of Greece—Pericles or Alexander the Great?

ALPHABET JUMBLE

An ancient alphabet table fell and broke into pieces. Help historians by matching our modern-day letters to each of the Phoenician and Greek pairs. The first one has been done for you.

Phoenician	Greek	Modern
1. 𝘡	Ι	J
2. Υ	Υ	
3. ♯	Α	
4. ᒑ	Ρ	
5. φ	G	
6. ◁	Δ	
7. ᒧ	Γ	
8. ᕓ	Β	
9. ↓	Κ	
10. ᵞ	Μ	
11. Υ	F	
12. ᔕ	Ν	
13. Υ	Υ	

Phoenician	Greek	Modern
14. W	Σ	
15. 𝘡	Ι	
16. ᒥ	Γ	
17. Ο	Ο	
18. ᒧ	Γ	
19. Υ	Υ	
20. ⋆	Δ	
21. ╤	Χ	
22. ᒐ	Λ	
23. ᴲ	F	
24. Ι	Ζ	
25. +	Τ	
26. Υ	Υ	

MYTHOLOGY MYSTERIES

Identify the character from Greek mythology. Write the name on the line after the description.

1. She challenged Athena to a spinning and weaving contest. Because of her arrogance, she was changed into a spider._____

2. He stole fire from Mount Olympus and brought it to man. For this he was severely punished by Zeus._____

3. She was a forest nymph protecting Zeus from his jealous wife Hera. Hera cursed the nymph's voice so that she could only repeat what was spoken to her._____

4. According to the myth, his god rides his golden chariot across the sky each morning to usher in the new day._____

5. The king of the gods, he was famous for his relationships with several women. He fathered several gods and heroes in mythological tales._____

6. She was a powerful goddess, worshipped by many. The myth of her birth is that she sprouted straight out the head of Zeus, full-grown._____

7. In order to please a vengeful king, this hero performed twelve remarkable labors, including battles against fierce and unusual creatures._____

8. When his lover died, this hero could not bear to be without her, so he traveled to the Underworld to bring her back. His beautiful music helped him persuade Hades to let her go._____

9. He was the king of Cyprus who carved a stone statue of a beautiful maiden. He fell in love with the statue, and the gods brought the statue to life._____

10. One of the many sons of Zeus, this hero's accomplishments include killing the snake-haired Medusa and turning giant Atlas to stone._____

11. She was a jealous wife. One myth tells how she turned her husband's lover into a cow guarded by a 100-eyed monster. When the monster was killed by Hermes, she put the hundred eyes onto the peacock's feathers._____

12. Considered the most beautiful goddess of all she sprang from the sea foam and rode ashore on a giant scallop shell._____

13. In the myth of the seasons Hades kidnapped her daughter so that her mourning turned the earth barren. During the time that her daughter returns, the earth springs back to life._____

14. He sailed on a ship called the Argos in search of the Golden Fleece._____

GOVERNMENT GRAB BAG

Like other civilizations, the ancient Greeks tried several different forms of government before becoming a democracy. Match each word in the box below to its description.

1. A ruler who has total power not limited by a constitution or other officials, this person usually seizes power and is an oppressive ruler._____

2. The aristocracy, or people in the upper class or high ranks._____

3. A self-governing unit made up of a city and its surrounding villages and farmland._____

4. An organizational structure that resembles a pyramid, with one person at the top and many people at the bottom. People at each level supervise those in the level below them._____

5. A territory governed as a unit within a country or empire._____

6. An economic system in which nobles own the farmland and peasants work it._____

7. A ruler with absolute power and authority and whose word must be obeyed._____

8. The policy and practice of forming and maintaining an empire characterized by the subjugation and control of territories and the establishment of colonies within an ever-expanding area._____

9. A nation in which political power lies with the citizens who elect leaders and representatives. The head of state in this form of government is not a king._____

10. A system of government in which a king, queen, or emperor is the sole and absolute ruler. A ruler is chosen based on heredity rather than election._____

11. A system of government in which the people rule, either directly or through their elected representatives._____

12. A nation and the other nations it has conquered. A political unit often made up of several nations under one leadership._____

13. A series of rulers from the same family._____

14. A system of government in which a few people rule over the entire population._____

15. The overthrow of a government or social system with another taking its place._____

monarchy	revolution	city-state
province	empire	republic
bureaucracy	dictator	imperialism
tyrant	oligarchy	nobility
dynasty	feudalism	democracy

DRAW A FAMOUS GREEK STATUE

Use the clues below to draw a famous Greek statue using the enlarged grid on the following page.

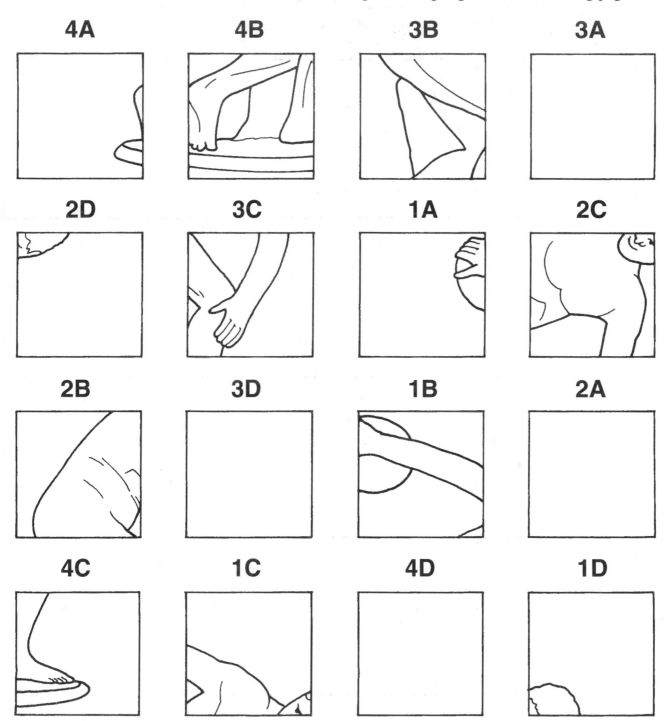

4A   4B   3B   3A

2D   3C   1A   2C

2B   3D   1B   2A

4C   1C   4D   1D

DRAW A FAMOUS GREEK
STATUE *(cont.)*

	A	**B**	**C**	**D**
1				
2				
3				
4				

ATHENS OR SPARTA?

Write an "A" for Athens or a "S" for Sparta in each blank.

_____ 1. The economy was based on agriculture and trade.

_____ 2. The people believed in simple luxury for themselves and their homes. Most excess money went to help improve the city-state.

_____ 3. Governed by an oligarchy run by five ephors and a 30-man senate, these 35 men truly made all decisions for the city-state although there was a public assembly.

_____ 4. The women did not participate in public life or own property. They took their status from their husbands and were only allowed to accompany them publicly to the theater or religious festivals.

_____ 5. Only noncitizens had occupations outside the military, including trade, farming, and crafts.

_____ 6. Girls were allowed to marry between 15 and 20 years of age. The government encouraged them to have more than one husband so they could produce more children for the military.

_____ 7. The people believed in the beauty of mind, body, and spirit, which required vigorous exercise at the gymnasium, relaxation in the public baths, and stimulating conversation at the Agora.

_____ 8. At one time its large slave population revolted. So this city-state created a strong army dominated by a harsh lifestyle and vigorous training. The people were so devoted to patriotism that the government controlled all aspects of family life.

_____ 9. All citizens, regardless of social class, participated in making decisions for this government run by a democracy.

_____10. Boys of wealthy citizens entered private school at the age of six, accompanied by a tutor or pedagogue. They lived at home until the age of 18 when they joined the military.

_____11. The government gave each citizen a plot of land which was worked by state slaves called helots.

_____12. The basis of its economy was the military and its conquests. Military work was the only occupation allowed for male citizens.

ATHENS OR SPARTA? *(cont.)*

Write an "A" for Athens or a "S" for Sparta in each blank.

_____13. The people required few luxury goods since they believed that a dependence on comfort weakened the spirit.

_____14. Family life was controlled by the father. Boys were released from any parental authority at the age of 21.

_____15. Girls were considered adults at age 12 or 13. At that time they married and began having families and running households of their own.

_____16. The city-state prospered during the Golden Age under the leadership of Pericles. The Acropolis was built to protect and beautify the city.

_____17. New babies were inspected by the government. If the government felt they were healthy and strong, the babies remained with the family. Otherwise, the government took the baby and put it outside the city to die.

_____18. Boys joined the military barracks from ages 7–18 and did not live with their families. Their training involved terrible hardships in which they ate little, wore few clothes, endured pain, and spoke few words. All of these things were to strengthen their minds and bodies.

_____19. Different citizens pursued different occupations, depending on their family trade, such as farming, trading, and crafting.

_____20. Girls and women were athletic and competed in sports to create healthy mothers who would bear healthy children.

_____21. Girls did not receive a formal education nor did they participate in athletic competition. Instead, they were taught to run a household by their mothers and were educated in reading, writing, math, music, literature, and dance.

_____22. Although families lived together, there were separate quarters for men, women, slaves, and children.

_____23. Women had many freedoms and were considered full citizens. They could own land or run their own businesses, but they could not vote in the assembly or join the military.

_____24. Males did not gain full citizenship until the age of 30. At that time they were allowed to marry, but they were not home much because they were constantly training or fighting in battles.

OLYMPIC NUMBERS

Write the correct numbers on the lines.

1. The first official Olympics occurred in _____. Although the games had been taking place for many years previously, this was the first year in which winners were actually documented.

2. The very first Olympic games consisted of only one event, a footrace _____ long.

3. Still, the first Olympic games drew a crowd of over _____ spectators.

4. The Olympic games were held in tribute to Zeus, and athletes competed every _____ years.

5. In Olympia, where the games were held, there stood a _____ -foot statue of Zeus made of gold and ivory. It is considered one of the Seven Wonders of the Ancient World.

6. As the Olympics grew more popular, athletes from all over the world came to compete. To qualify, they were required to arrive _____ days prior to the games for training.

7. Soon, more and more events were added to the competition. By the 6th century B.C., there were _____ different events.

8. One of the more exciting events was a chariot race in the Hippodrome, a flat arena with a post at each end. The racers had to make _____ turns around the posts, which meant they covered about 5 ¹/₂ miles.

9. Another popular event was the pentathlon. The winner was the athlete who completed _____ of _____ different events.

10. Although the games were mainly a man's sport, boys from the ages of _____ to 17 were allowed to compete.

11. The Olympics were held for over _____ years.

12. In the year _____ Emperor Theodosius of Rome put an end to the games, claiming they went against the spirit of Christianity, the official religion of the Roman Empire at the time.

TAKE ME TO YOUR LEADER

Answer these questions about Rome's top leaders to decode one of the most famous quotes in history. Write the letters of your answers on the blanks of the corresponding question's number.

"__ __   __ __   __ __ __ __ __?"
  1 4   2 7   3 8 5 9 6

1. When did Julius Caesar cross the Rubicon River and change the history of Rome forever?

   47 B.C.=R   **48 B.C.=E**

2. This young leader fell in love with Queen Cleopatra and eventually had children with her. His death was said to be the cause of her suicide.

   Mark Antony=T   **Julius Caesar=E**

3. He took control of the Western Roman Empire after the death of his great uncle. He then fought to become the sole ruler of the entire Empire when he learned that Egypt was to gain part of the Eastern Empire.

   Mark Antony=T   **Octavian=B**

4. Julius Caesar was killed on the steps of the Senate for fear he was becoming too powerful. How was he killed?

   Stabbed with daggers=T   **Beaten with stones=U**

5. The last ruler of the Julio-Claudian dynasty died in disgrace. During his rule the Zealots rebelled in Judea and a great fire swept through Rome. Rather than assuming the responsibility for the neglect of his duties, he blamed the fire on the Christians. Who was this man?

   Titus=T   **Nero=U**

6. While still a young soldier, this leader was captured by pirates, held for ransom, and lived to boast about it. Who was this man?

   Hadrian=C   **Julius Caesar=E**

7. Augustus Caesar ruled the Roman Empire and began a period of peace known as the Pax Romana. When did his great reign end?

   A.D. 14=U   **A.D. 20=S**

8. During the reign of Titus from A.D. 79–81, which great volcano erupted, burying the cities of Pompeii and Herculaneum?

   Mount Vesuvius=R   **Mount Olympus=E**

9. Around A.D. 300, this ruler created one of the worst waves of persecution against the Christians in history. He destroyed churches, burned books and crosses, fired Christians from jobs, removed them from the military, and killed many Christians. Who was this man?

   Constantine=B   **Diocletian=T**

Answer these questions about the quote above.

10. Who said these words and in what language? _____

11. When and where were these words spoken? _____

12. Tell what the quote means in English and what the person meant when he said it. _____

_____

ALL MIXED UP

In the boxes, write the correct names for the Roman and Greek gods. Note: One name repeats for both the Roman and Greek name.

- Pluto
- Artemis
- Demeter
- Hermes
- Bacchus
- Diana
- Athena
- Mars
- Hestia
- Aphrodite
- Venus
- Zeus
- Neptune
- Mercury
- Minerva
- Vesta
- Hera
- Dionysus
- Apollo
- Hephestus
- Hades
- Poseidon
- Jupiter
- Vulcan
- Juno
- Ceres
- Ares

Roman Name	Greek Name	Description
		1. Goddess of the harvest
		2. God of light, truth, and healing
		3. Goddess of love and beauty
		4. Goddess of wisdom and war
		5. God of war and violence
		6. Goddess of the hearth
		7. God of the forge
		8. Queen of the gods
		9. God of the dead and the Underworld
		10. God of wine and fertility
		11. Goddess of the hunt and the moon
		12. Messenger of the gods
		13. King of the gods
		14. God of the seas

IT'S THE FASHION

People in Ancient Rome did strange things to enhance their appearances. Some social rules were equally bizarre. Write the correct word in each blank.

1. To soften _____, apply a cream of wheat flour and donkey milk, or use crushed snails.

2. For _____ skin, apply lead paste or powdered chalk.

3. To define _____, use a needle to apply crushed ant's eggs or ashes.

4. Curl _____ with heated tongs, apply oil with earthworm ashes to keep it from turning gray.

5. To dye hair _____, use lentils, wine, and cypress leaves boiled with leeks.

6. To make hair _____ faster, use bear fat or the ashes from hippopotamus skin.

7. To get rid of _____ hair, use tweezers or bat's blood and hedgehog ashes.

8. If you are a _____ of 16, wear a toga virilis.

9. A galeri is a fashionable _____ worn by women.

10. Senators display a crescent on the _____ of their boots.

11. Use the triclinium, or _____ room, for parties.

12. Guests bring their own _____ to use when dining and to carry home food _____.

13. Slaves cater to every guest, even by _____ meat into bite-sized pieces.

14. Between courses everyone _____ to be ready to enjoy the next foods served.

boy	eyebrows	cutting	hairpiece
pale	napkins	toe	hair
black	vomits	dining	leftovers
grow	skin	arm	

FUN IN ROME

Unscramble the following words and phrases.

1. ubpilc outfninas _____

2. asdram _____

3. toracs _____

4. toiharc versrid _____

5. sucriC masuMix _____

6. emags _____

7. madistu _____

8. adenc meparnorcef _____

9. itenga nad kningdrik _____

10. veslas _____

11. oldboy bactom _____

12. drinen typra _____

13. mufro _____

14. comk baltest _____

15. certnocs _____

16. lagidarots _____

17. cersdan _____

18. dwil ebsats _____

19. tethera _____

20. tosep _____

21. Oplcymsi _____

22. giorusel stiflasev _____

23. anare _____

24. tabeshouh _____

25. toricha cesra _____

26. sicmusani _____

27. tesaleth _____

FUN IN ROME *(cont.)*

Write each word or phrase from page 36 in the proper category.

Places for Socializing and Entertainment	Types of Entertainment	The Entertainers

GRID PATTERN MOSAIC

The Romans decorated their floors with intricate patterns of cut tile. Duplicate a Roman mosaic on page 39 by connecting the coordinates listed below. Then color the pattern, cut it out, and combine it with other classmates' panels to create a large mosaic.

Mosaic Coordinates

(0,6) to (2,8)	(7,4) to (8,5)
(0,5) to (3,8)	(8,5) to (9,4)
(1,4) to (2,5)	(9,4) to (8,3)
(2,5) to (3,4)	(8,3) to (7,4)
(3,4) to (2,3)	(7,0) to (10,3)
(2,3) to (1,4)	(8,0) to (10,2)
(0,3) to (3,0)	(7,8) to (10,5)
(0,2) to (2,0)	(8,8) to (10,6)
(3,6) to (5,4)	(4,7) to (4,6)
(5,4) to (7,6)	(4,6) to (5,5)
(7,6) to (7,5)	(5,5) to (6,6)
(7,5) to (6,4)	(6,6) to (6,7)
(6,4) to (7,3)	(6,7) to (5,8)
(7,3) to (7,2)	(5,8) to (4,7)
(7,2) to (5,4)	(4,2) to (4,1)
(5,4) to (3,2)	(4,1) to (5,0)
(3,2) to (3,3)	(5,0) to (6,1)
(3,3) to (4,4)	(6,1) to (6,2)
(4,4) to (3,5)	(6,2) to (5,3)
(3,5) to (3,6)	(5,3) to (4,2)

GRID PATTERN MOSAIC *(cont.)*

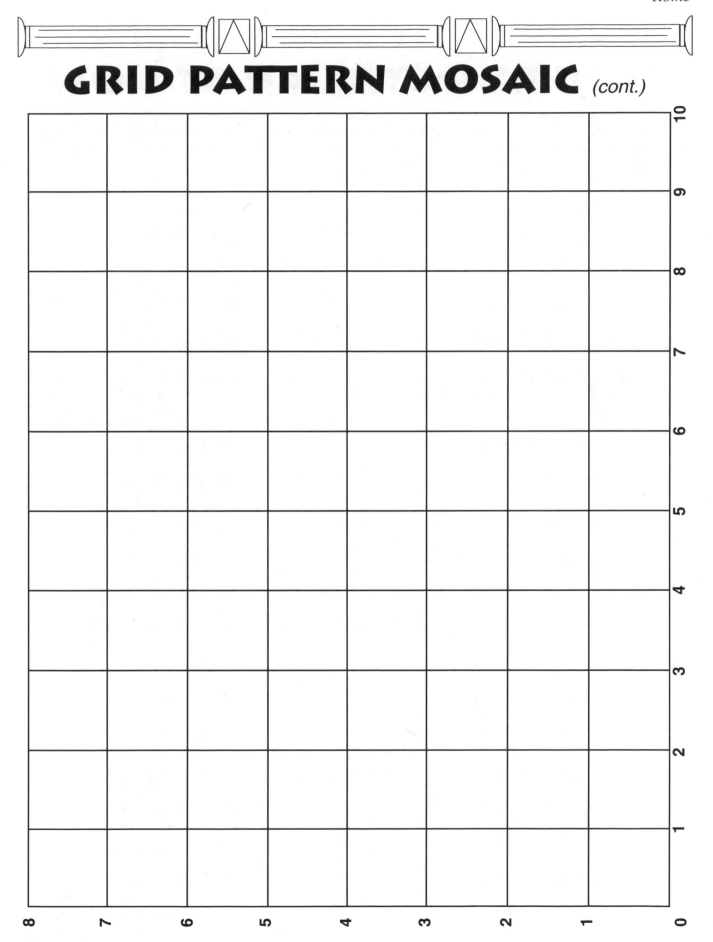

YOU'RE IN THE ARMY NOW

Use words from the box below to complete the statements about military life in ancient Rome. You may use some words more than once and some not at all.

1. A citizen of Rome who joined the military became a _____ .

2. Upon signing for military duty, soldiers pledged an oath of loyalty to the _____ and vowed to serve for _____ years.

3. Noncitizens entering the military would join the ranks of the _____ .

4. The basic uniform of a Roman soldier was a red _____ tunic under a vest of armor.

5. The armor was made from _____ strips connected by _____ straps.

6. Military sandals were designed for long marches and made from _____ .

7. A _____ helmet was worn, designed to protect the head, _____ , and side of the face.

8. One-third of a soldier's wages went towards rationed food. A soldier kept his money in a _____ purse that he tied to his _____ .

9. Standard weapons included a dagger worn on the _____ , a javelin, a shield, and a short stabbing sword called a _____ .

10. One of the best defensive maneuvers was forming a _____ , or tortoise. Soldiers locked their shields together to form a circular dome.

11. While on a military expedition, soldiers lived in _____ tents. During periods of peace they helped to build _____ forts.

12. If a soldier proved himself worthy in battle, eventually he might climb the ranks and become a _____ in charge of a unit of approximatly 100 soldiers.

• 25	• reed	• centurion
• wooden	• leather	• emperor
• the gods	• 15	• metal
• legionary	• belt	• gladius
• testudo	• canvas	• neck
• wrist	• auxiliaries	• arm
• woolen	• shoulder	

KNOW YOUR LATIN

Research the definitions of the underlined Latin words or phrases. Circle the letter of the correct response.

1. You were called a ***particeps criminis*** as you left the bank. What should you do?
    A. Get a good lawyer   B. Open a new account   C. Go home and shower

2. You have been taken to the ***post partum*** room at the hospital. What did you just do?
    A. Died of a heart attack   B. Had a baby   C. Had your appendix removed

3. You have been asked to give an ***impromptu*** speech. What will you do?
    A. Read from your notes   B. Demonstrate a task   C. Speak without preparation

4. You have bought a ***bona fide*** purebred dog. What is it?
    A. A mixed breed dog   B. A real pure breed dog   C. An inbred dog

5. You are told that the dress code at your school is ***status quo***. What does this mean?
    A. Unchanged   B. Mandatory   C. What the majority wear

6. You have been served a ***subpoena***. What do you have?
    A. A long sandwich   B. A naval induction   C. A summons to appear

7. You just graduated from college ***cum laude***. How do your parents feel?
    A. Broke   B. Disappointed   C. Proud

8. Your friend is coming to the mall ***incognito***. What will she be wearing?
    A. A disguise   B. An army combat uniform   C. The latest fashion

9. You want to bring your ***alter ego*** to the movies with you. Whom are you bringing?
    A. Your most trusted friend   B. Your sibling   C. Your spouse

10. You awoke this morning with a feeling of ***vertigo***. How do you feel?
    A. Nauseous   B. Dizzy   C. Sleepy

11. The consequences for your actions are established ***ex post facto***. When will you learn the consequences?
    A. Before you act   B. Before the facts are known   C. After you act

12. You can go to the concert if you get a ***consensus*** from your friends' parents. What do you need?
    A. An agreement   B. A ride   C. A head-count of those going

ROMAN NUMERALS

Number the alphabet with A=1, B=2, C=3, etc. Translate each Roman numeral into an Arabic number. Then turn each number into a letter to spell out the clue words below. The first letter has been done for you.

1.	P̄ XVI 16	I	VII	I	XIV	XIX			
2.	III	VIII	XVIII	IX	XIX	XX	IX	I	XIV
3.	XVI	V	XVIII	XIX	V	III	XXI	XX	IX	XV	XIV
4.	IV	IX	XV	III	XII	V	XX	IX	I	XIV
5.	XIX	I	III	XVIII	IX	VI	IX	III	V	IXX
6.	XII	IX	XV	XIV	XIX				
7.	XIII	I	XVIII	XX	XXV	XVIII	XIX		
8.	III	I	XX	I	III	XV	XIII	II	XIX
9.	III	XV	XIV	XIX	XX	I	XIV	XX	IX	XIV	V
10.	XIX	I	XII	XXII	I	XX	IX	XV	XIV

ROMAN NUMERALS *(cont.)*

Use the words from page 42 to complete the following statements about the Romans and the Christians.

The 1. _____ were people who did not believe in one god. This

included the majority of the Roman people, as well as the people in the extended Empire.

Most Roman authorities ignored the 2. _____ people who did not

interfere. It wasn't until problems began to arise in the Empire that they were used as

scapegoats. Waves of cruel 3. _____ against Christians and Jews

continued for hundreds of years. The worst happened under the leadership of

4. _____. Stories tell of human 5. _____ in

which Christians were thrown into the arena with wild 6. _____ if

they refused to convert and worship Roman gods and emperors. These Christians who gave

up their lives were considered 7. _____ . They were given special

places within the 8. _____ for burial. Some of their tombs were

turned into shrines to give hope to other Christians. Eventually, a Roman ruler came into

power who was sympathetic to the Christians. His name was 9. _____.

His rule was a type of 10. _____ for Christians, and under his

leadership Christianity became the official religion of the Roman Empire.

HINDU NAME GAMES

Use the first part of each word to create the names of some Hindu gods.

1. shine + vacation = _____

2. during + game = _____

3. inside + drapes = _____

4. Brahams + mattress = _____

5. again + nice = _____

6. gangster + gather = _____

7. party + vaccine + time = _____

Match each of the following Hindu gods to the animal he or she is depicted as riding.

8. Agni   A. white elephant

9. Ganesha   B. ram

10. Brahma   C. snake

11. Indra   D. swan

12. Vishnu   E. bull

13. Durga   F. red lion

14. Shiva   G. mouse

Write the names of the gods that fit these descriptions.

15. god of the sky, rain, and thunder _____

16. the preserver _____

17. god of fire _____

18. wife of Lord Shiva _____

19. the destroyer _____

20. Ganges River goddess _____

21. the creator _____

22. goddess of war, birth, and death _____

      44

CONNECT HINDU-ARABIC NUMBERS

Use the chart at the bottom of the page to convert the ancient Hindu-Arabic numbers to counting numbers. Then complete the dot-to-dot of an Indian icon. "X" marks a new starting point.

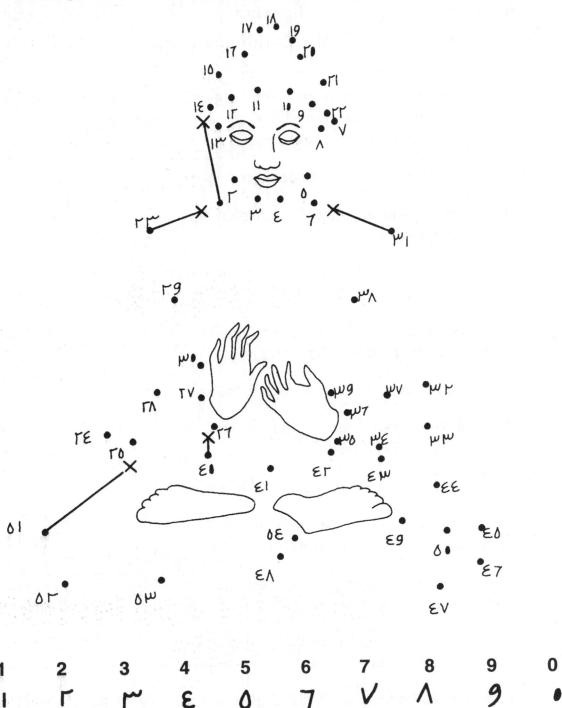

1	2	3	4	5	6	7	8	9	0
١	٢	٣	٤	٥	٦	٧	٨	٩	٠

FASCINATING FACTS ABOUT FAITHS

Match each fact to the correct Indian religion. Some facts fit more than one religion.

H = Hinduism	**I = Islam**	**C = Christianity**
S = Sikhism	**B = Buddhism**	**J = Jainism**

_____ 1. Fanatic followers of this religion endure great pain to worship their god. They lie on beds of nails, starve themselves, and stare at the sun until they are blind. Some carry around bones and drink from skulls.

_____ 2. Five hermits were the first disciples of this religion.

_____ 3. This religion believes in the reincarnation of one's life spirit into other living things after death.

_____ 4. Followers of this religion practice yoga and meditation to free their minds and reach the absolute.

_____ 5. The founder of this religion was said to have emerged from the right side of his mother as she grasped a flowering tree.

_____ 6. The name of this religion means both "submission to God" and "peace."

_____ 7. The people of this religion eventually broke off from the rest of India to form their own country called Pakistan.

_____ 8. This religion practices fasting for certain religious holidays.

_____ 9. In this religion, the men never cut their hair and grow beards. They all use the same last name which means "lion."

_____ 10. This religion uses writings comprised of historical accounts, verses, hymns, instructions, proverbs, legends, and tales to help pass on its teachings.

_____ 11. Some female followers of this religion practice "sati" or ritual suicide by sitting on their deceased husbands' burning funeral pyres.

_____ 12. In his youth, the founder of this religion was a prince leading a sheltered life. He questioned the meaning of life and his destiny in India.

FASCINATING FACTS ABOUT FAITHS *(cont.)*

_____13. This religion believes in treating others the way you would wish to be treated yourself.

_____14. Twelve disciples helped foster this religion.

_____15. The founder of this religion is said to have received the word from God through an angel named Gabriel.

_____16. After the founder's death, followers of this religion set out to convert followers in neighboring lands by using military force.

_____17. Followers of this religion sweep the paths in front of them and wear masks over their mouths so that they don't harm any living creature, even a bug or germ.

_____18. This religion was founded by a man attempting to unite the Muslims and Hindus in India.

_____19. Followers of this religion believe strongly in one god.

_____20. This religion gained more followers after the execution of its main founder.

_____21. Many people in this religion are vegetarians, since eating meat would be considered an act of violence against animals.

_____22. Followers of this religion must adhere to strict rules about worship, prayer, and pilgrimage.

_____23. Followers of this religion do not believe in one personal god. Instead, they believe in obtaining perfect wisdom through the right faith, the right knowledge, and the right conduct.

_____24. This religion does not believe in equality and places people in a specified social status from birth until death.

_____25. In this religion, it is said that the mother of the founder was told by an angel that she was pregnant. The baby was not her husband's since she was a virgin but instead belonged to God.

India

REGIONS AND CULTURES MAP

In the late sixth century, India split into independent kingdoms and states. Match the following kingdoms with their locations.

Telugu	Tamil	Bengali	Sindhi	Pashto	Kashmiri
Baluchi	Nepali	Sinhalese	Kannada	Marathi	Dzongka
Oriya	Punjabi	Hindi	Gujarati	Malayalam	Assamese

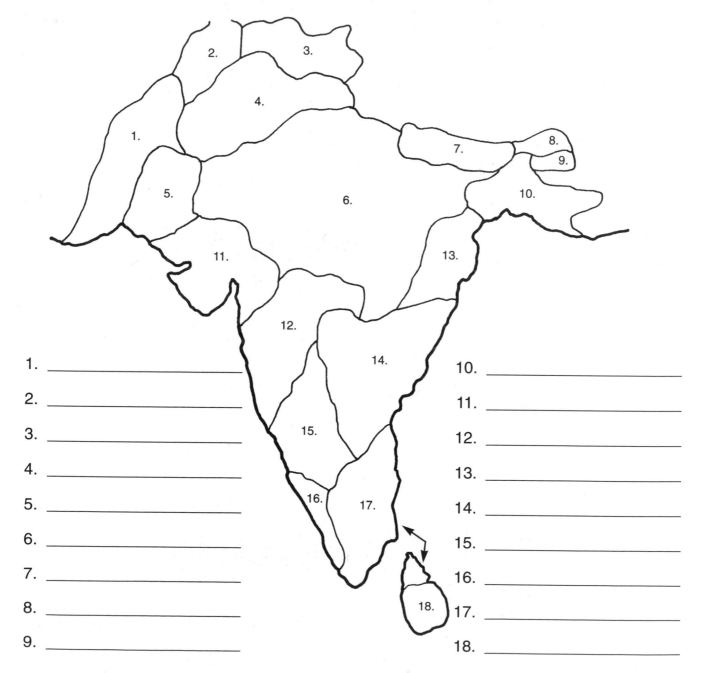

1. _____

2. _____

3. _____

4. _____

5. _____

6. _____

7. _____

8. _____

9. _____

10. _____

11. _____

12. _____

13. _____

14. _____

15. _____

16. _____

17. _____

18. _____

WONDERS OF INDIA

The mysterious resources of India drew explorers from all over the world. Find and circle 30 of India's most precious plants, animals, minerals, and spices. Words are spelled frontwards and backwards either horizontally, vertically, or diagonally.

```
E  L  T  O  R  T  O  I  S  E  S  L  R  A  E  P
N  M  I  L  E  S  N  R  A  P  E  A  C  O  C  K
A  A  N  D  P  L  O  E  A  L  S  N  T  B  R  L
C  N  O  I  P  S  M  G  X  I  L  O  N  S  E  I
R  G  N  I  E  T  A  I  C  U  R  R  Y  T  V  S
A  R  N  S  P  E  N  T  O  R  D  U  G  O  L  D
G  O  N  R  K  I  N  D  A  O  G  I  D  N  I  B
U  V  E  A  V  A  I  P  O  N  D  V  R  E  S  A
S  E  N  S  H  N  C  W  L  O  V  O  I  S  A  N
D  S  A  P  I  A  L  M  A  G  O  R  N  E  N  Y
R  L  E  A  M  A  O  P  F  A  T  Y  D  L  D  A
I  L  O  E  D  M  V  S  F  M  I  E  C  I  R  N
E  U  L  N  R  O  E  L  U  E  N  K  L  T  I  T
C  B  A  H  O  R  S  E  B  L  E  N  O  X  N  R
L  S  K  C  V  E  E  N  S  T  U  O  T  E  T  E
U  T  L  I  O  N  O  T  T  O  C  M  E  T  I  E
```

- banyan tree
- buffalo
- bull
- camel
- cinnamon
- cloves
- cotton
- curry
- deer
- elephant
- gold
- horse
- indigo
- ivory
- lion
- mangroves
- monkey
- parrot
- peacock
- pearls
- pepper
- rice
- sandalwood
- silk
- silver
- snake
- stones
- sugarcane
- tiger
- tortoise

WHAT DO YOU KNOW?

Fill in the blanks with a name, place, or key concept. You may use reference books or other resources to complete this page.

1. The first and greatest civilization in ancient India developed near the valley of the Indus River around 3000 B.C. The _____ was larger than any other ancient empire, including those of Egypt and Mesopotamia.

2. The two largest centers of this civilization were _____ and _____ .

3. This civilization eventually declined as another group of people called _____ migrated into India around 1500 B.C. and began the Vedic Age.

4. These people brought the Sanskrit language with them and famous epic tales of courage.

   One such tale is _____.

5. The mingling ideas from the Aryan and Indus Valley religions formed the basis of _____ , which is still the most popular religion in India today.

6. This religion adopted the Aryan concept of a _____ that dictated a person's social class at birth. Regardless of one's actions, a person could not change his or her social status and so remained in a particular class until death.

7. A main source of information about the Aryan religion comes from a document called the _____ , a collection of hymns, poems, and verses used in religious ceremonies.

8. One of the greatest religious leaders was born about 560 B.C. His real name was _____ and he was the son of a king. After his long path towards enlightenment he became known as _____ . His religion appealed to many because it did not recognize the Aryan caste system.

9. During the sixth century B.C., the _____ moved into northwest India, and the region of Gandhara became part of this vast empire.

10. However, in 327 B.C., _____ conquered the region and claimed it for Greece.

11. While the Greeks influenced life in northwestern India, another great empire was forming in central India. In about 321 B.C., a young prince named _____ seized power and founded the _____ Empire.

12. This empire reached its height under the grandson of its founder. _____ came to the throne in 269 B.C. and soon controlled the majority of Indian territory. A main source of information about his reign comes from stone inscriptions called _____ .

13. After the Mauryan Empire dissolved, India split into a number of independent kingdoms. It wasn't until A.D. 320 that the second great empire emerged—the _____ . During this period culture flourished, and it is often referred to as the _____ Age of India.

14. _____ was one of the royal poets during this age.

BUDDHA'S LIFE

Sequence the following events in the proper order.

_____ 1. The young prince grew up sheltered from life outside the kingdom walls. He was trained to be a great king and excelled in all of his studies, yet was never quite content.

_____ 2. After reaching enlightenment under the bodhi tree, Buddha sought out the five hermits and taught them the Four Noble Truths he had discovered and the Eightfold Path to follow. The hermits then became Buddha's first disciples and helped spread his word.

_____ 3. Upon hearing the dream, the wise men of the kingdom predicted the queen would give birth to a son who would become a great king or leave and become a holy man.

_____ 4. After meeting the monk, Siddhartha decided to leave his riches, his family, and his protected life in order to seek Truth and find peace.

_____ 5. Soon the prediction came true, and the queen gave birth to her son in the royal garden. The boy was named Siddhartha, meaning "every wish fulfilled." Seven days later, the queen died.

_____ 6. Siddhartha sat in meditation for 49 days under the bodhi tree. At dawn on the 50th day, Siddhartha became enlightened.

_____ 7. During his search for Truth, Siddhartha joined five hermits who denied their bodies comfort. He remained with them for six years, eating little and enduring great pain.

_____ 8. After preaching for 45 years, Buddha died at the age of 80. Having reached enlightenment, he then entered a state known as nirvana, his soul never to come to earth again.

_____ 9. One night while a queen slept in her kingdom, she had a dream. A beautiful elephant with six golden tusks came to her, gently touching her right side with a lotus blossom.

_____10. The night Siddhartha was to leave the palace for his quest, his wife gave birth to a baby boy.

_____11. On his second venture outside the kingdom, Siddhartha met a monk who seemed at peace.

_____12. Upon reaching 16, Siddhartha married a beautiful princess. Three exquisite palaces were built in the hope that Siddhartha would remain in the kingdom. Yet, after 13 years of easy living, he only grew more restless.

_____13. After denying his body comfort for six years with the hermits, Siddhartha decided to follow a middle path and live in moderation. He ate, bathed, and sat beneath a bodhi tree to meditate.

_____14. Finally, out of curiosity, Siddhartha ordered his driver to take him outside the kingdom walls. For the first time the prince witnessed human suffering, sickness, and death.

DYNASTY DYNAMICS

Place the name of the correct dynasty after each set of dates.

- Tang
- Yuan
- Song

- Qing
- Shang
- Ming

- Qin
- Sui
- Han
- Zhou

1. 1788–1027 B.C _____
2. 1027–256 B.C. _____
3. 221–207 B.C. _____
4. 207 B.C.–A.D. 220 _____
5. A.D. 589–618 _____

6. A.D. 618–906 _____
7. A.D. 960–1279 _____
8. A.D. 1279–1368 _____
9. A.D. 1368–1644 _____
10. A.D. 1644–1912 _____

Calculate the number of years each dynasty ruled. List them in the chart, from the dynasty with the longest rule to that with the shortest rule.

	Dynasty	Duration
11.		
12.		
13.		
14.		
15.		
16.		
17.		
18.		
19.		
20.		

THE GREAT WALL

Use the word and number bank below to complete these statements about the Great Wall of China. Not all words will be used to fill in the blanks.

1. The Great Wall is China's most _____ landmark and is made of only dirt and _____ .

2. It is the longest structure ever made by _____ and the only one that can be seen from _____ with the naked eye.

3. The wall runs nearly _____ miles along China's _____ border.

4. The wall was built to _____ China from its enemies in the north and to keep farmers from leaving China to pursue a _____ lifestyle.

5. Emperor Qin (Chin) ordered the wall built in 214 B.C. It took more than _____ men to connect the various _____ that form the wall.

6. It took hundreds of thousands of men _____ years to build the wall.

7. These men were drafted, fed little, and worked hard. Many of them died from starvation and _____ .

8. Because of the toll of human life it took, the wall was nicknamed "The longest _____ on Earth."

9. Still, the wall is an architectural wonder. It is _____ feet high, _____ feet wide at its base, and _____ feet wide at the top.

10. A road along the top of the wall can fit _____ horses side-by-side.

11. Soldiers traveled this road. Many stood guard at the _____ watchtowers set _____ feet apart.

12. Messages were sent the length of the wall using _____ , mirrors, and _____ signals.

• humans	• 2,500	• northern	• sections
• machines	• famous	• 30	• metal
• southern	• Mars	• stone	• 5
• 40,000	• telegraph	• 750	• attack
• cemetery	• 25	• protect	• exhaustion
• space	• nomadic	• smoke	• 300,000
• runners	• bricks	• 15	• 10

NAME THE INVENTION

Match the Chinese invention or product to its description.

_____	A. kung fu	_____	F. paper
_____	B. wheelbarrow	_____	G. compass
_____	C. fireworks	_____	H. water clock
_____	D. kites	_____	I. chopsticks
_____	E. silk	_____	J. printing

1. For hundreds of years the Chinese kept how to make this a secret, but eventually the process was smuggled out of the country. It is made from the cocoon of a caterpillar that feeds on mulberry leaves.

2. In A.D. 105, Cai Lun, a civil servant, invented this. He used silk rags, mulberry bark, bamboo, and hemp. These items were boiled, mashed, and pounded to create the finished product.

3. These items, made from silk, bamboo, and eventually paper, were invented more than 2,500 years ago and used by soldiers of the Han dynasty to scare away enemies.

4. Chinese doctors may have accidentally discovered this invention while searching for a way to cure illnesses. Made from potassium nitrate, sulfur, and charcoal, these were used to scare away evil spirits and ghosts.

5. The ancient Chinese called this a "south pointing fish," since the original invention consisted of a wooden fish with a piece of metal floating in a bowl of water.

6. Designed over 2,000 years ago, the Chinese "wooden ox" or "gliding horse" helped laborers in the country and city. It took Europeans over 1,300 years to learn of this product and copy it.

7. In A.D. 1090 a civil servant named Su Song presented the emperor with the first model of this invention. It took four years to build and stood over 30 feet tall. Run by a paddle wheel and water, it caused gongs and bells to ring every 15 minutes.

8. This was created during the Tang dynasty by an artisan who carved the surface of a wooden block in the form of a Chinese character, or symbol for a word.

9. These have been used throughout the Orient for more than 3,000 years. It is considered rude to point with them or to leave them sticking up in a bowl, as this resembles incense placed before a grave.

10. Many forms of this are used around the world. One style, known as wing chun, was invented by a nun and is based upon the movements of the crane and snake.

ANCIENT CHINA IN NUMBERS

Write the correct number in each blank.

1. It takes 40,000 silkworms to produce _____ pounds of silk.

2. Written Chinese history began with simple pictographs that date back _____ years.

3. Today the Chinese language contains over _____ symbols or characters.

4. Paper making was discovered in A.D. _____ by a Chinese civil servant.

5. Printing was invented during the Tang dynasty, and the earliest printed book dates to A.D. _____ .

6. The Old Silk Road spans _____ miles west to the Mediterranean.

7. The Chinese built the longest canal in the world, stretching _____ miles from Tianjin to Hangzhou.

8. Genghis Khan took control of Yanjing (Beijing) in A.D. _____ , and his grandson Kublai Khan ruled all of China by A.D. _____ .

9. Marco Polo astounded European readers with his exotic accounts of China. He served as a valued official in China for nearly _____ years.

10. China was ruled by a series of dynasties for _____ years.

11. The last dynasty was destroyed by a revolution in A.D. _____ .

12. Emperors enjoyed a separate life in the royal Forbidden City, which contained _____ buildings for good luck.

13. An extravagant ruler named Shi Huangdi had _____ clay soldiers buried with him for protection in his afterlife. Remarkably, each face is different.

14. The Chinese calendar has _____ months and is based on the phases of the moon.

6,000	1271	750
2,133	8,000	563
40,000	2,500	105
1279	10	12
1912	1,000	9,999
13	30	20
4,000	551	1215
868	6	

CONFUCIUS SAYS

Answer the following questions about Confucius.

1. In 551 B.C. Confucius was born. His real name was ___ ___ ___ ___
   7
   ___ ___ ___ ___ ___.
   11

2. Confucius was born into a family of minor ___ ___ ___ ___ ___ ___ and grew to be a
   5   15
   respectful son.

3. He lived during a time of constant ___ ___ ___ ___ ___ ___ ___ in China, uncertain
   1   11
   whether the fighting would reach his family.

4. Instead of joining the military as a soldier, he studied for a
   ___ ___ ___ ___ ___ ___ ___ ___ ___ ___ job.
   2   3

5. He later finished his education and became a ___ ___ ___ ___ ___ ___ ___.
   3   12

6. Confucius taught his pupils a set of ___ ___ ___ ___ ___ for proper living rather than
   7   14
   preaching a religion.

7. Although Confucianism was not a religion, he taught purity, sincerity, self-respect,
   ___ ___ ___ ___ ___ ___ ___ for others, and how to follow proper rituals to reach
   13   3
   these goals.

8. Respect for superiors and respect for ___ ___ ___ ___ ___ ___ ___ by their children
   4   14
   was a large part of his teachings which dealt with proper relationships among people for
   keeping order in society.

9. In each relationship the superior person's duty was to look after the inferior person,
   whose job it was to follow and ___ ___ ___ ___.
   15 18

10. He advised ___ ___ ___ ___ ___ ___ ___ to rule by setting a good example rather
    9   14
    than setting harsh laws and punishments.

11. He did not support the system of dynasties for running the
    ___ ___ ___ ___ ___ ___ ___ ___ ___.
    8   17

12. Instead, he argued that the government should be run by the most
    ___ ___ ___ ___ ___ ___ ___ ___ ___ people with high moral character and
    9   6   6
    education.

13. During his lifetime, Confucius drew little ___ ___ ___ ___ ___ ___ ___ ___ ___ for
    10   5
    his accomplishments.

14. Still, during the 400 years of the Han Dynasty, Confucianism became the official doctrine
    or ___ ___ ___ ___ ___ ___ of China.
    16 18

CONFUCIUS SAYS *(cont.)*

Use the number clues from page 56 to decode a famous saying of Confucius.

—— —— —— —— —— —— ——   —— —— —— —— —— —— —— ——,
1   6   3   12   2   7   3   9   10   4   13   5   6   5   8

—— —— ——   —— —— —— ——   —— —— —— —— —— ——
3   12   10   1   6   14   10   15   10   16   2   17   10

—— —— —— —— —— —— ——;   —— ——
11   2   2   9   6   14   12   15   18

—— —— —— —— —— —— —— ——,   —— —— ——
9   10   4   13   5   6   5   8   3   12   10

—— —— —— —— —— —— ——   —— —— —— —— —— ——
11   2   2   9   6   14   12   15   10   16   2   17   10

—— —— —— ——.
1   6   14   10

CHINESE NEW YEAR

Research this popular holiday to fill in the missing words.

Chinese New Year is the most important 1. _____ or celebration in China. The date varies because it is based on the 2. _____ calendar. The celebration began as a spring festival. Before the spring 3. _____ China's farmers gave thanks for the renewed fertility of the 4._____. Today, Spring Festival is a time to pay debts, settle 5. _____ , and make a fresh start for the new year. Chinese people traditionally do many things to prepare for the New Year's celebration, hoping that the coming 6. _____ will be the best and most prosperous year yet. Before New Year's 7. _____ , the house is completely 8. _____ . People sweep their houses, clearing away the 9. _____ to let in health and happiness. Men and boys get their hair 10. _____ and buy new 11. _____ so that they are also "new" for the new year. When New Year's Eve comes, all of the 12. _____ must be paid. The New Year's celebration lasts 13. _____ days, although the Spring Festival will continue until the 15th day of the new year. These days are spent eating holiday 14. _____ and visiting family and 15. _____ . On the first day of the new year, children receive a 16. _____ envelope from loving adults. The color stands for joy and 17. _____ during the coming year. When children open the envelopes, they find 18. _____ that is always given in 19. _____ amounts. When the adults visit each other during the celebration days, they take oranges or tangerines, 20. _____ , and candy with them and present them to the owner of the house. The owner may not 21. _____ all of the gifts, sometimes returning 22. _____ of whatever is given him or extending another gift in return. This shows that they will share and help their friends during the coming year. The green 23. _____ on the tangerines stand for 24. _____ . As a gift this means the recipients are wished a happy life. The last day of the New Year's celebration is a very happy day with huge paper 25. _____ and lions p arading through the streets and 26. _____ exploding. Both are used to scare 27. _____ spirits away for another year.

ROOSTER

BOAR

DRAGON

RAT

CHINESE ZODIAC

The twelve animals of the Chinese zodiac are below. Unscramble the names of each animal and calculate the missing dates by adding or subtracting 12 years. Find your birth year, and read the traits the Chinese attribute to your sign.

1. **BBARIT** _____1951, _____, 1975, _____

   Lucky, talented, clever, forgiving, articulate, affectionate, shy, peace-seeking

2. **EASNK** _____1953, _____, _____, 1989

   Wise, intense, physically beautiful, somewhat vain, high tempered, and decisive

3. **NOADRG** _____,1963, 1976, _____

   Lucky, generous, eccentric, complex, passionate, and healthy

4. **HSPEE** _____1943, _____, _____, 1979

   Elegant, creative, shy, prefer anonymity

5. **ESORH** _____, 1966, _____, 1990

   Popular, attractive, friendly, athletic, sometimes impatient

6. **YOMNKE** _____, 1956, 1968,_____

   Intelligent, influential, enthusiastic, achiever, funny, somewhat easily discouraged

7. **OSORETR** _____1945, _____, 1969, _____

   Pioneer spirit, devoted to work, popular, eccentric, somewhat selfish

8. **TRA** _____, 1960, 1972, _____

   Ambitious, energetic, honest, good sense of humor, good friend, sometimes spends too freely

9. **GRETI** _____1950, _____, 1974, _____

   Strong, aggressive, courageous, candid, and sensitive

10. **XO** _____, 1961, _____, 1985

    Bright, patient, an inspiration to others, gentle, and peace-loving

11. **ORAB** _____1947, _____, _____, 1983

    Loyal, sincere, sensitive, noble, and chivalrous

12. **GDO** _____, 1958, _____, 1982

    Loyal, honest, team player, courageous, smart, generous, sometimes stubborn

MAGIC SQUARES

The Chinese were fascinated by numbers and played this game called "magic squares." Using the numbers between 1 and 9 only once, put a number in each box so that when each set of numbers is added vertically, horizontally, or diagonally they equal 15.

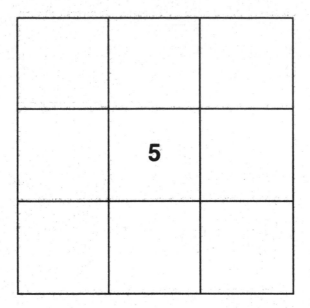

Use the two magic squares below to try other numbers in the middle box. Remember to use each number only once and make sure all sets of numbers add to 15. Once you have discovered an entire square, challenge a friend.

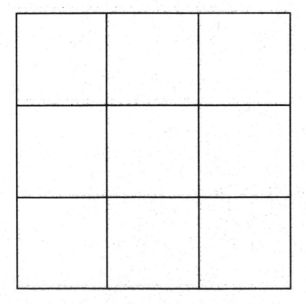
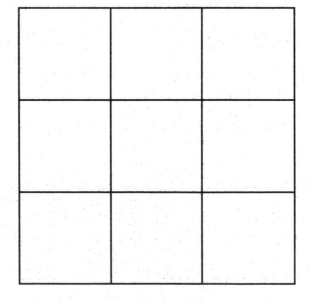

FAMOUS LAST WORDS

Match the person from the list below with his or her alleged last words.

_____ 1. "Decay is inherent in all component things."

_____ 2. "Go to the rising sun, for I am setting. Think more of death than of me."

_____ 3. "To the strongest!"

_____ 4. "Remember my last saying: show kindness to your friends then you shall have it in your power to chastise your enemies."

_____ 5. "If our time be come, let us die manfully for our brethren, and let us not stain our honor."

_____ 6. "Et tu Brute?"

_____ 7. "Let us ease the Romans of their continual dread and care, who think it long and tedious to await the death of a hated old man."

_____ 8. "Crito, I owe a cock to Asclepius. Will you remember to pay the debt?"

_____ 9. "Little urn, you will soon hold all that will remain of him whom the world could not contain."

_____ 10. "No intelligent monarch arises. There is no one in the kingdom that will make me his master. My time has come to die."

_____ 11. "The play is over."

_____ 12. "Oh Allah, be it so."

_____ 13. On finding an asp in a bowl of fruit, "So here it is!"

_____ 14. "It is finished."

_____ 15. "For it is not right that in the house of song there be mourning. Such things befit us not."

A. Cyrus the Great, of Persia, died 529 B.C.
B. Septimus Severus, died A.D. 211
C. Hannibal of Carthage, suicide 183 B.C.
D. Sappho (Greek poet), died c. 600 B.C.
E. Confucius, died 479 B.C.
F. Mohammed, died A.D. 632
G. Augustus Caesar, died A.D. 14
H. Cleopatra of Egypt, suicide 30 B.C.
I. Julius Caesar, assassinated 44 B.C.
J. Judas Maccabaeus, killed in battle 160 B.C.
K. Socrates, forced suicide 399 B.C.
L. Buddha, died 483 B.C.
M. Jesus of Nazareth, executed A.D. 33
N. Alexander the Great, died 323 B.C.
O. Marcus Aurelius, died A.D. 180

16. List the letters in chronological order from the earliest person's death to latest person's death. _____

_____

_____

ANCIENT PROVERBS

Match these ancient proverbs to their meanings.

Proverb

1. Although the owl has large eyes, he can't see as well as a mouse.
2. The cherry tree is known among others by its flowers.
3. Ice coming from water is colder than water.
4. Boat-swallowing fish do not live in brooks.
5. A protruding stake will be hammered in.
6. Although shrimps may dance around, they do not leave the river.
7. Unless you enter the tiger's den you cannot take the cubs.
8. A cornered rat will bite a cat.
9. Great trees are envied by the wind.
10. Fish do not live in clear water.
11. Though the wind blows, the mountain does not move.
12. Everywhere the crows are black.

Meaning

_____ A. Prominent people in business, politics, and intellectual life are often attacked by lesser people.

_____ B. Be self-disciplined so that you are indifferent to any tumult or disturbance.

_____ C. A talented person stands out among his fellows.

_____ D. A person should not leave his occupation but work according to his specified position in life.

_____ E. Cramped circumstances do not produce greatness.

_____ F. Size does not necessarily mean efficiency.

_____ G. Even the weak when at bay may defeat the strong.

_____ H. Nothing ventured, nothing gained.

_____ I. A child might surpass a parent, master, or teacher in skill.

_____ J. All people everywhere have the same principles in the conduct of life, so we must always act honorably toward others.

_____ K. Deceit and dishonesty are a necessary part of the environment of people who wish to succeed in the world.

_____ L. It is wiser at times to lie low than to be forward, for the latter will certainly cause trouble.

LATIN TODAY

Latin was the most widely used language around the ancient world. Match the following definitions to these commonly used Latin words and phrases of today.

1. et cetera _____
2. quasi _____
3. ad arbitrium _____
4. quid pro quo _____
5. habeas corpus _____
6. per se _____
7. ipso facto _____
8. per diem _____
9. vice versa _____
10. ad hoc _____
11. contra _____
12. carpe diem _____
13. ergo _____
14. gratuitus _____
15. re _____
16. ante delictum _____
17. interdum _____
18. per capita _____

A. now and then
B. conversely
C. by itself, intrinsically
D. this for that
E. without cost
F. before the crime
G. at will
H. therefore
I. by the day, each day
J. and so forth
K. as it were
L. opposite
M. for each individual
N. to this
O. by that very fact
P. legal detention, have the body
Q. seize the day
R. regarding

Find and write the meanings of these Latin words.

19. duplex _____

20. ovum _____

21. emporium _____

22. homicide _____

23. femur _____

24. genesis _____

25. cerebrum _____

ANCIENT GEOGRAPHY

Use an atlas to find the ancient city at the given locations

Name of City	**Civilization**	**Latitude/Longitude**	
1. _____	Israel	32° N	25° E
2. _____	Roman	41° N	29° E
3. _____	Assyria	37° N	43° E
4. _____	Greece	35° N	25° E
5. _____	Syria	34° N	36° E
6. _____	China	40° N	116° E
7. _____	Greece	31° N	30° E
8. _____	Sumeria	31° N	46° E
9. _____	India	26° N	85° E
10. _____	Egypt	30° N	31° E
11. _____	Roman	41° N	29° E
12. _____	Greece	37° N	22° E
13. _____	Phoenicia	34° N	36° E
14. _____	Israel	32° N	35° E
15. _____	Babylonia	33° N	45° E
16. _____	India	31° N	73° E
17. _____	Phoenicia	37° N	10° E
18. _____	Roman	42° N	13° E
19. _____	Egypt	25° N	33° E
20. _____	China	34° N	109° E

ANCIENT GEOGRAPHY *(cont.)*

Fill in the missing information about these major rivers in the ancient world.

River	Empire	Length
1. _____	China	5,464 km
2. Yangtze (Chang Jiang)	_____	6,300 km
3. Nile	Egypt	_____
4. _____	Mesopotamia	1,899 km
5. Euphrates	_____	2,430 km
6. Indus	India	_____
7. _____	India	2,511 km
8. Danube	Greece	_____

Unscramble the following mountains and desserts of the ancient world. Then write the civilization that defined the area.

	Name	Civilization
9. TONUM MOLSUPY	_____	_____
10. PSAL	_____	_____
11. ASINI SETERD	_____	_____
12. SAYLAMAHI	_____	_____
13. BANARIA TEREDS	_____	_____
14. THAGS	_____	_____
15. BANINU RESTED	_____	_____

IMPORTANT B.C. DATES

Research to find the dates B.C. for these major events in history.

_____1. The first recorded Olympic games were held in Greece.

_____2. The code of Hammurabi, one of the first law codes, was drawn up and displayed.

_____3. The Sumerians developed cuneiform writing.

_____4. A number of small cities, the world's first civilization, appeared in Sumer of Mesopotamia.

_____5. The pyramids and Sphinx were built in Giza, Egypt.

_____6. Sargon of Akkad united all Mesopotamia under his rule, creating the world's first empire.

_____7. The Hebrews founded a kingdom under the leadership of David in what is now Palestine.

_____8. The people of Rome revolted against their Etruscan rulers and established a republic.

_____9. Moses led the Hebrews on an exodus from Egypt into the Sinai desert.

_____10. Buddha was born as Siddhartha Gautama in northern India.

_____11. Alexander the Great defeated the Persians, opening the way to his conquest of northern India.

_____12. The Han dynasty began its 400-year rule in China.

_____13. The Indus Valley civilization began to flourish in the cities of Mohenjo-Daro and Harappa.

_____14. The Shang Dynasty began its rule in the Huang He Valley of China.

_____15. King Menes of Upper Egypt united Lower and Upper Egypt.

_____16. Cyrus the Great established the Persian Empire.

_____17. Judaism was founded by Abraham.

_____18. The Romans conquered Greece.

_____19. The Qin dynasty established China's first strong central government.

_____20. Augustus became the first Roman emperor.

IMPORTANT A.D. DATES

Write the correct date on the blank before each event.

_____1. Mohammed, the founder of Islam, began his preaching.

_____2. Cleopatra and Mark Antony ruled Egypt for Rome.

_____3. Egypt became a Muslim nation.

_____4. A group of Jews called "Zealots" revolted against Roman rule.

_____5. The Pax Romana ended with the death of the last emperor, Marcus Aurelius.

_____6. A great fire swept through Rome during the reign of Nero. He blamed the fire on the Christians and ordered them killed.

_____7. Arabs conquered the area around the Indus Delta and brought Islam to India.

_____8. The Han Empire fell in China. There was a period of warfare between the states for over 350 years.

_____9. China was finally united again as an Empire after 350 years of fighting.

_____10. The Western Roman Empire fell to Germanic tribes.

_____11. Jesus was crucified by Roman authorities.

_____12. The Chinese invented paper.

_____13. The Roman Empire was split into the Byzantium Empire in the East and the Western Roman Empire.

_____14. Constantine granted freedom of religion and ended all persecution of the Christians. Christianity became the official religion of the Roman Empire shortly thereafter.

_____15. India flourished in its Golden Age under the Gupta dynasty.

1st century	180	476
33	220	589
64	313	610
66	320	650
105	395	711

IMPORTANT PEOPLE IN ANCIENT HISTORY

2600s B.C.–700s B.C.

Match the correct name from the list and write the letter on the blank before the description.

A. Wu   **F.** Abraham   **K.** David

B. Hatshepsut   **G.** Sargon of Akkad   **L.** Hammurabi

C. Aenas   **H.** Yu   **M.** Moses

D. Minos   **I.** Homer   **N.** Thutmose III

E. Chang Tang   **J.** Imhotep

_____1. An Egyptian military leader and pharaoh who expanded the borders of Egypt, he was nephew to Queen Hapshepsut.

_____2. The Chinese ruler whose defeat of Chieh in 1766 B.C. began the Shang dynasty.

_____3. He was the first documented leader of the Israelite nation.

_____4. He was a Mesopotamian ruler and creator of the world's first true empire.

_____5. The founder of Xia, the first great Chinese dynasty.

_____6. He Israelite king led the defeat of the Philistines and the growth of the Israelite Empire. He captured Jerusalem and made it the capital.

_____7. A female pharaoh in Egypt worked on trade expeditions and beautifying Egypt. She created monuments and famous obelisks.

_____8. He was an adviser to the ancient Egyptian king Zoser and designer of the first Step Pyramid.

_____9. According to legend, this Trojan hero escaped to Italy, where his son Romulus founded Rome.

_____10. This Babylonian ruler created one of the first codes of written law. This code was posted on an obelisk for all to see and covered rights for all people.

_____11. This Greek was an epic poet and author of the *Iliad* and the *Odyssey.*

_____12. This Hebrew led the Israelites out of Egyptian captivity and gave them the Ten Commandments from God.

_____13. The ruler of the Zhou dynasty finally conquered the Shang.

_____14. He was the legendary king of Crete during its cultural height. He built the Palace at Knossos that became the labyrinth in the myth *Theseus and the Minotaur.*

IMPORTANT PEOPLE IN ANCIENT HISTORY

700s B.C.–170 B.C.

Match the correct name from the list and write the letter on the blank before the description.

A. Asoka

B. Confucius

C. Mo-Tzu

D. Nebuchadnezzar

E. Hannibal

F. Darius

G. Socrates

H. Qin Shihuangdi (Cheng)

I. Plato

J. Han Gaozu

K. Alexander the Great

L. Buddha

M. Sappho

N. Pericles

_____1. A Chinese philosopher and teacher at the end of the Zhou dynasty, his teachings became the doctrine of China.

_____2. This famous Greek philosopher was a student of Socrates.

_____3. This Buddhist ruler of the Mauryan Empire in India posted edicts throughout his empire to convey his ruling philosophy.

_____4. This was the Chinese founder of Moism, a philosophy that stressed universal love.

_____5. This King of Babylon conquered the Phoenicians, Philistines, and Hebrews and exiled them from the land.

_____6. This Carthaginian general fought against the Romans in the Second Punic War.

_____7. This Persian king led the war against the Greek city-states, forcing Athens and Sparta to work together.

_____8. This Indian philosopher and teacher founded the Buddhist religion.

_____9. The Athenian military and political leader brought Greece into its prosperous Golden Age.

_____10. This Greek philosopher was accused of corrupting Athenian youth with his teachings. He killed himself by drinking hemlock.

_____11. This great Greek poet founded a school for girls.

_____12. The was the most famous emperor of the Qin dynasty and unifier of ancient China. Under his rule, the Great Wall of China was built, and the name "China" comes from his name. In his tomb archaeologists found 8,000 clay soldiers.

_____13. This was the first emperor of the Han dynasty in China, which began the revival of Confucianism and combined it with Legalism to run the government.

_____14. This Macedonian king conquered Greece, Persia, and Egypt. He established his empire's capital, Alexandria, in Egypt, where he built a grand library and lighthouse.

IMPORTANT PEOPLE IN ANCIENT HISTORY

c. 170 B.C.–A.D. 500s

Match the correct name from the list and write the letter on the blank before the description.

A. Attila the Hun   **F.** Antiochus   **K.** Pontius Pilate

B. Alaric   **G.** Wudi   **L.** Jesus

C. Brutus   **H.** Spartacus   **M.** Julius Caesar

D. Diocletian   **I.** Augustus Caesar   **N.** Constantine

E. Nero   **J.** Chandra Gupta II

_____1. This leader of the group of Roman Senators assassinated Julius Caesar in 44 B.C.

_____2. This king of a tribe of barbarians conquered Roman cities, helping to cause the fall of the Roman Empire.

_____3. During the reign of this greatest of Gupta kings, the Golden Age of India reached its peak. The famous poet Kalidasa was part of his court.

_____4. This Roman emperor installed Christianity as the main religion in the Empire and moved the capital to Constantinople.

_____5. This Visigoth king was credited with the major invasions that conquered the Roman Empire.

_____6. This unpopular Roman emperor was the last ruler of the Augustan dynasty. He blamed the Christians for the great fire that demolished Rome.

_____7. This Roman emperor reformed the empire and imposed severe Christian persecution.

_____8. This Syrian ruler's orders for the Jews to worship Greek gods led to the Maccabean revolt.

_____9. This Roman slave led a successful slave uprising in 73 B.C.

_____10. This Roman governor ordered the execution of Jesus in A.D. 33.

_____11. Given the title "respected one" by the Roman Senate, his actual name was Octavian, and he ruled as the first Roman Emperor.

_____12. This Chinese emperor ruled the Han dynasty and expanded the empire into southern China, North Vietnam, and North Korea. He sent the first trade expeditions into the west, which resulted in the growth of the Silk Road.

_____13. This Roman general ended the Republic and ruled as a dictator from 46–44 B.C. He was assassinated on the steps of the Senate.

_____14. A Hebrew teacher and founder of Christianity he was executed by Roman officials.

WONDERS OF THE ANCIENT WORLD

Write the name of the civilization that created these amazing structures.

- Mesopotamia
- Egypt
- Greece

- Rome
- India
- China

1. Colosseum _____

2. Red Fort _____

3. Great Wall _____

4. Zeus at Olympia _____

5. Appian Way _____

6. The Acropolis _____

7. Ajanta Caves _____

8. Ziggurat _____

9. Alexandria Lighthouse _____

10. Pyramids of Giza _____

11. Temple of Artemis _____

12. Hanging Gardens _____

13. Forum _____

14. Taj Mahal _____

15. Hippodrome _____

16. Sphinx _____

17. Parthenon _____

18. Abu Simbel _____

BURIAL IN THE ANCIENT WORLD

Place the words at the bottom of the page dealing with death and burial in the appropriate civilization's box.

Egypt

Greece

Rome

India

China

- Cerebus the 3-headed guard dog
- Osiris and Anubis
- shabtis
- cremation with funeral pyre
- Christian martyrs
- mummification
- gold coin placed under tongue
- jade to prevent body decay

- cremation ashes placed in urn
- King Tut's golden mask
- the catacombs
- reincarnation
- opening of the mouth ceremony
- Field of Reeds
- cemeteries outside city walls
- ashes in the Ganges River

- Tartarus ruled by Hades
- sati or ritual suicide by wife
- weighing of the heart
- burial in a grave shaped like a cross
- 8,000 clay soldiers buried with emperor
- crossing the River Styx
- The Elysian Fields

FASHION IN THE ANCIENT WORLD

Place the words at the bottom of the page dealing with fashion in the appropriate civilization's box.

Egypt	**Greece**

Rome	**India**	**China**

- chiton
- cashmere
- double crown
- wax pomade on wig
- false beard
- toga virilis
- red fingernails
- white face powder
- red forehead dot

- wedding band showing clasped handsquilted jacket
- cotton pants and shirt
- intricate henna hands/feet patterns
- red ankh on palm
- paddy hat
- headband
- shenti
- false hair curls

- sari
- culottes
- pigtails
- peplos
- turban
- braided wig
- chintz
- silk dresses
- long mustache

ANCIENT WORLD WORD GAME

Play this game with a partner. Words or names must relate to an ancient civilization. Players take turns writing a word or name that starts with any letter that has not been used. Allow three minutes for a player to fill in a word. If a player cannot write a word in the alotted time, play passes to the other player. Play continues until neither player can fill in a word. The player who wrote the most words is the winner. Play again with the same or a different partner. Do not repeat any of the words used in the first game.

	Game 1	Game 2	Game 3
A			
B			
C			
D			
E			
F			
G			
H			
I			
J			
K			
L			
M			
N			
O			
P			
Q			
R			
S			
T			
U			
V			
W			
X			
Y			
Z			

ANSWER KEY

Page 3
1. Fertile Crescent
2. Jordan River
3. Cyprus
4. Tigris River
5. Hattusa
6. Red Sea
7. Mount Sinai
8. Babylon
9. Mediterranean Sea
10. Arabian Desert
11. Dead Sea
12. Mesopotamia

Page 4
1. wheeled vehicles
2. sailboats
3. irrigation systems
4. dikes
5. canals
6. copper tools
7. bronze weapons
8. jewelry
9. pottery wheel
10. bricks
11. cuneiform writing
12. mythology
13. calendar
14. clock minutes
15. units of measurement

Page 5
1. Babylonians
2. Sumerians
3. Phoenicians
4. Hittites
5. Assyrians
6. Hittites
7. Babylonians
8. Sumerians
9. Hebrews
10. Sumerians
11. Babylonians
12. Hebrews
13. Phoenicians
14. Sumerians

Page 6
1. Solomon
2. Zealots
3. David
4. Gideon
5. Judas
6. Maccabees
7. Moses
8. Samson
9. Goliath
10. Saul
11. Jesus
12. Herod
13. Esther
14. Daniel
15. Joshua
16. Ruth
17. Abraham
18. Noah
19. Philistines
20. Samaritans
21. Mary
22. Dalilah
23. Pharisees
24. Israelites

Page 7
Hammurabi's Code
B,C,F,H,K,L,M
Hebrew Law
A,D,E,G,I,J

Page 8
In an open mouth, a fly enters.

Page 9
1. These two rivers formed the fertile crescent area known as Mesopotamia. These two rivers allowed the formation of the first civilizations in the world.
2. These two architectural wonders were created by the ancient Babylonians during the reign of King Nebuchadnezzar from 605–562 B.C.
3. These were the three forms of written language that allowed the spread of civilization, trade, and commerce throughout the world.
4. These two historical figures recorded their people's sets of laws onto stone for the first time.
5. Two famous Sumerian figures, they are included in some of that civilization's most famous epic tales.
6. Three metals were discovered that were put to use in the ancient world for tools, weapons, and ornamentation. These three metals brought humans into a new era of discovery and technology.
7. These two basic forms of transportation were invented by the Sumerians and then built upon by following civilizations.
8. These two leading cities in Phoenicia organized and controlled trade throughout the Mediterranean.
9. Three capitals of ancient Mesopotamia, they were where great civilizations grew.
10. Three major bodies of water surrounding the Middle East region, they offered trade with and protection from outlying areas.

Page 10
1. King Gilgamesh
2. Ashurbanipal
3. Moses
4. Nebuchadnezzar
5. Abraham
6. Hattusili II
7. King David
8. Hammurabi
9. Ibbi-Sin
10. Antiochus
11. Sir Leonard Woolley
12. Hiram the Great

Page 11
1. C
2. B
3. I
4. E
5. A
6. F
7. D
8. G
9. L
10. J
11. H
12. K

Page 16
1. Ramses
2. Cleopatra
3. Akhenaten
4. Tutankhamen
5. Hatshepsut
6. Khufu
7. Zoser
8. Ramses
9. Thutmose
10. Cleopatra
11. Hatshepsut
12. Menes
13. Zoser
14. Khufu
15. Akhenaten
16. Tutankhamen

Page 18
1. site
2. foundation
3. geometry, west
4. level, water
5. dirt
6. base
7. limestone, logs
8. Nile
9. sleds

ANSWER KEY (cont.)

10. capstone
11. top, polish, base

To have a stairway to heaven.

Page 19

O my heart, do not stand as witness against me! Do not oppose me in the judgment. Do not be hostile to me in the presence of the Keeper of the Balance.

This is the weighing of the heart ceremony.

Page 20

1. brain
2. mummy
3. heart
4. oils and spice
5. incision
6. chest
7. resin
8. natron
9. priest
10. mask
11. flax
12. tomb
13. mummification
14. canopic jars
15. palm wine
16. abdomen
17. internal organs
18. sarcophogus
19 All terms are about the mummification process.

Page 21

1. sheaths, pleated gold
2. shentis, waists, knots
3. sandals, reed, thong
4. wigs, vegetable, cloth
5. oils, skin
6. plucked, painted, kohl
7. lines, glare
8. ochre, animal fat
9. henna, toenails, feet
10. gems, tied, neck

Page 22

1. Zeus
2. Ares
3. Hermes
4. Hera
5. Athena
6. Hades
7. Hestia
8. Apollo
9. Demeter

Page 23

Everyone is equal before the law.

Page 24

1. Thessaly
2. Crete
3. Ionian Sea
4. Sparta
5. Minoan Age
6. *Iliad*
7. monarchy
8. slaves
9. Delphi
10. Zeus
11. Dionysus
12. Persian Wars
13. Parthenon
14. Pericles
15. Alexander the Great

Page 25

1. J
2. U,V,W,Y
3. H
4. R
5. Q
6. D
7. P
8. B
9. K
10. M
11. F
12. N
13. U,V,W,Y
14. S
15. I,J
16. C,G
17. O
18. C,G
19. U,V,W,Y
20. A
21. X
22. L
23. E
24. Z
25. T
26. U, V, W, Y

Page 26

1. Arachne
2. Prometheus
3. Echo
4. Apollo
5. Zeus
6. Athena
7. Hercules
8. Orpheus
9. Pygmalion
10. Perseus
11. Hera
12. Aphrodite
13. Demeter
14. Jason

Page 27

1. tyrant
2. nobility
3. city-state
4. bureaucracy
5. province
6. feudalism
7. dictator
8. imperialism
9. republic
10. monarchy
11. democracy
12. empire
13. dynasty
14. oligarchy
15. revolution

Page 29

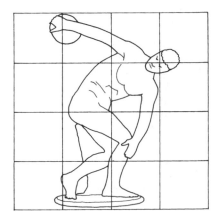

Pages 30–31

1. A		13. S	
2. A		14. A	
3. S		15. A	
4. A		16. A	
5. S		17. S	
6. S		18. S	
7. A		19. A	
8. S		20. S	
9. A		21. A	
10. A		22. A	
11. S		23. S	
12. S		24. S	

Page 32

1. 776 B.C.
2. 200 meters
3. 45,000
4. 4
5. 40
6. 30
7. 13
8. 12
9. 3, 5
10. 12
11. 1,000
12. A.D. 394

ANSWER KEY (cont.)

Page 33

1. E
2. T
3. B
4. T
5. U
6. E
7. U
8. R
9. T
10. Julius Caesar, Latin
11. On the steps of the Senate as he was stabbed.
12. "You too, Brutus?" Caesar was surprised and dismayed to find his good friend Brutus wanted him dead.

Page 34

1. Ceres, Demeter
2. Apollo, Apollo
3. Venus, Aphrodite
4. Minerva, Athena
5. Mars, Ares
6. Vesta, Hestia
7. Vulcan, Hephestus
8. Juno, Hera
9. Pluto, Hades
10. Bacchus, Dionysus
11. Diana, Artemis
12. Mercury, Hermes
13. Jupiter, Zeus
14. Neptune, Poseidon

Page 35

1. skin
2. pale
3. eyebrows
4. hair
5. black
6. grow
7. arm
8. boy
9. hairpiece
10. toe
11. dining
12. napkins, leftovers
13. cutting
14. vomits

Page 36

1. public fountains
2. dramas
3. actors
4. chariot drivers
5. Circus Maximus
6. games
7. stadium
8. dance performance
9. eating and drinking
10. slaves

11. bloody combat
12. dinner party
13. forum
14. mock battles
15. concerts
16. gladiators
17. dancers
18. wild beasts
19. theater
20. poets
21. Olympics
22. religious festivals
23. arena
24. bathhouse
25. chariot races
26. musicians
27. athletes

Page 37

Places for Socializing and Entertainment
public fountains
stadium
dinner party
forum
theater
arena
bathhouse

Types of Entertainment
dramas
Circus Maximus
games
dance performance
eating and drinking
bloody combat
mock battles
concerts
Olympics
religious festivals
chariot races

The Entertainers
actors
chariot drivers
slaves
gladiators
dancers
wild beasts
poets
musicians
athletes

Page 39

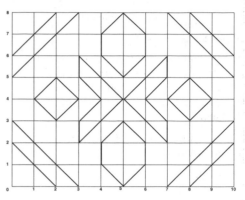

Page 40

1. legionary
2. emperor, 25
3. auxiliaries
4. woolen
5. metal, leather
6. leather wrist
7. metal, neck
8. leather, wrist
9. belt, gladius
10. testudo
11. leather, wooden
12. centurion

Page 41

1. A
2. B
3. C
4. B
5. A
6. C
7. C
8. A
9. A
10. B
11. C
12. A

Page 42

1. pagans
2. Christian
3. persecution
4. Diocletian
5. sacrifices
6. lions
7. martyrs
8. Catacombs
9. Constantine
10. salvation

Page 43

1. pagans
2. Christian
3. persecution
4. Diocletian

5. sacrifices
6. lions
7. martyrs
8. catacombs
9. Constantine
10. salvation

Page 44

1. Shiva
2. Durga
3. Indra
4. Brahma
5. Agni
6. Ganga
7. Parvati
8. ram-B
9. mouse-G
10. swan-D
11. white elephant-A
12. snake-C
13. red lion-F
14. bull-E
15. Indra
16. Vishnu
17. Agni
18. Parvati
19. Shiva
20. Ganga
21. Brahma
22. Durga

Page 45

Pages 46–47

1. H
2. B
3. B,H,J,S
4. B,H
5. B
6. I
7. I
8. C,H,I
9. S
10. C,H,I,S
11. H
12. B,J

13. B,C,H,I,J,S
14. C
15. I
16. C,I
17. J
18. S
19. C,I,S
20. C
21. B,H,J
22. H,I,J
23. B,H,J
24. H
25. C

Page 48

1. Baluchi
2. Pashto
3. Kashmiri
4. Punjabi
5. Sindhi
6. Hindi
7. Nepali
8. Dzongka
9. Assamese
10. Bengali
11. Gujarati
12. Marathi
13. Oriya
14. Telugu
15. Kannada
16. Malayalam
17. Tamil
18. Sinhalese

Page 49

```
E L T O R T O I S E S L R A E P
N M I L E S N R A P E A C O C K
A N D P L O E A L S N T B R L
C N O I P S M G X I L O N S E I
R G N I E T A I C U R R Y T V S
A R N S P E N T O R D U G O L D
G O N R K I N D A O G I D N I A
U V E A V A I P O N D V R E S A
S E N S H N C W L O V O I S A N
D S A P I A L M A G O R N E N Y
R L E A M A O P F A T Y D L D A
I L O E D M V S F M I E C I R
E U L N R O E L U E N K L T I T
C B A H O R S E B L E N O X N E
L S K C V E E N S T U O T E T I
U T L I O N O T T O C M E T I E
```

Page 50

1. Indus Valley Civilization
2. Mohenjo Daro, Harappa
3. Aryans
4. Mahabharata
5. Hinduism
6. caste system
7. *Rig-Vedas*
8. Siddhartha Gautama, Buddha
9. Persians

10. Alexander the Great
11. Chandragupta, Mauryan
12. Asoka, edicts
13. Gupta Empire, Golden
14. Kalidasa

Page 51

1. 4
2. 13
3. 2
4. 8
5. 3
6. 12
7. 10
8. 14
9. 1
10. 9
11. 7
12. 5
13. 11
14. 6

Page 52

1. Shang
2. Zhou
3. Qin
4. Han
5. Sui
6. Tang
7. Song
8. Yuan
9. Ming
10. Qing
11. Zhou 771
12. Shang 761
13. Han 427
14. Song 319
15. Tang 288
16. Ming 276
17. Qing 268
18. Yuan 89
19. Sui 29
20. Qin 14

Page 53

1. famous, stone
2. humans, space
3. 2,500, northern
4. protect, nomadic
5. 300,000, sections
6. 10
7. exhaustion
8. cemetery
9. 30, 25, 15
10. 5
11. 40,000, 750
12. runners, smoke

Page 54

A. 10
B. 6

C. 4
D. 3
E. 1
F. 2
G. 5
H. 7
I. 9
J. 8

Page 55

1. 12
2. 6,000
3. 40,000
4. 105
5. 868
6. 4,000
7. 1,000
8. 1215, 1279
9. 20
10. 2133
11. 1912
12. 9,999
13. 8,000
14. 13

Page 56

1. Kung Futzu
2. nobles
3. warfare
4. government
5. teacher
6. rules
7. respect
8. parents
9. obey
10. leaders
11. government
12. qualified
13. attention
14. policy

Page 57

Without learning, the wise become foolish; by learning, the foolish become wise.

Page 58

1. festival
2. lunar
3. planting
4. soil
5. disputes
6. year
7. Eve
8. cleaned
9. old
10. cut
11. clothes
12. bills
13. four
14. foods

15. friends
16. red
17. good luck
18. money
19. even
20. cake
21. keep
22. half
23. leaves
24. life
25. dragons
26. firecrackers
27. evil

Page 59

1. rabbit, 1963, 1987
2. snake, 1965, 1977
3. dragon, 1951, 1988
4. sheep, 1955, 1967
5. horse, 1954, 1978
6. monkey, 1944, 1980
7. rooster, 1957, 1981
8. rat, 1948, 1984
9. tiger, 1962, 1986
10. ox, 1949, 1973
11. boar, 1959, 1971
12. dog, 1946, 1970

Page 60

row 1=8,3,4

row 2=1,5,9

row 3=6,7,2

Page 61

1. L
2. O
3. N
4. A
5. J
6. I
7. C
8. K
9. B
10. E
11. G
12. F
13. H
14. M
15. D
16. D, A, L, E, K, N, C, J, I, H, G, M, O, B, F

Page 62

1. F
2. C
3. I
4. E
5. L
6. D
7. H
8. G

9. A
10. K
11. B
12. J

Page 63

1. J
2. K
3. G
4. D
5. P
6. C
7. O
8. I
9. B
10. N
11. L
12. Q
13. H
14. E
15. R
16. F
17. A
18. M
19. double
20. egg
21. market
22. murder
23. thigh
24. beginning
25. brain

Page 64

1. Jerusalem
2. Constantinople
3. Nineveh
4. Knossos
5. Damascus
6. Beijing
7. Alexandria
8. Ur
9. Pataliputra
10. Memphis
11. Byzantium
12. Sparta
13. Byblos
14. Bethlehem
15. Babylon
16. Harappa
17. Carthage
18. Rome
19. Thebes
20. Xi'an

Page 65

1. Yellow River (Huang He)
2. China
3. 6671 km
4. Tigris
5. Mesopotamia
6. 2,900 km

7. Ganges
8. 2,858 km
9. Mount Olympus, Greece
10. Alps, Roman
11. Sinai Desert, Israel
12. Himalayas, China, India
13. Arabian Desert, Israel, Egypt
14. Ghats, India
15. Nubian Desert, Egypt

Page 66

(all dates are B.C.)

1. 776
2. 1700s
3. 3000
4. 3500
5. 2500
6. 2300
7. 1020
8. 509
9. 1200
10. 563
11. 331
12. 202
13. 2500
14. 1700
15. 3100
16. 550
17. 1700
18. 146
19. 221
20. 27

Page 67

(all dates are A.D.)

1. 610
2. 1st century
3. 650
4. 66
5. 180
6. 64
7. 711
8. 220
9. 589
10. 476
11. 33
12. 105
13. 395
14. 313
15. 320

Page 68

N 1. Thutmose III
E 2. Chang Tang
F 3. Abraham
G 4. Sargon of Akkad
H 5. Yu
K 6. David
B 7. Hatshepsut
J 8. Imhotep
C 9. Aenas

L 10. Hammurabi
I 11. Homer
M 12. Moses
A 13. Wu
D 14. Minos

Page 69

B 1. Confucius
I 2. Plato
A 3. Asoka
C 4. Mo-Tzu
D 5. Nebuchadnezzar
E 6. Hannibal
F 7. Darius
L 8. Buddha
N 9. Pericles
G 10. Socrates
M 11. Sappho
H 12. Quin Shihuangdi (Cheng)
J 13. Han Gaozu
K 14. Alexander the Great

Page 70

C 1. Brutus
A 2. Attila the Hun
J 3. Chandra Gupta II
N 4. Constantine
B 5. Alaric
E 6. Nero
D 7. Diocletian
F 8. Antiochus
H 9. Spartacus
K 10. Pontius Pilate
I 11. Augustus Caesar
G 12. Wudi
M 13. Julius Caesar
L 14. Jesus

Page 71

1. Rome
2. India
3. China
4. Greece
5. Rome
6. Greece
7. India
8. Mesopotamia
9. Greece
10. Egypt
11. Greece
12. Mesopotamia
13. Rome
14. India
15. Rome
16. Egypt
17. Greece
18. Egypt

Page 72

Egypt
mummification
Field of Reeds

weighing of the heart
Osiris and Anubis
opening of the mouth ceremony
shabtis
King Tut's golden mask
Greece
Tartarus ruled by Hades
gold coin placed under tongue
Crossing the River Styx
Cerebus the 3-headed guard dog
The Elysian Fields
Rome
cremation ashes placed in urn
the catacombs
Christian martyrs
cemeteries outside city walls
India
cremation with funeral pyre
sati or ritual suicide by wife
ashes in the Ganges River
reincarnation
China
jade to prevent body decay
8,000 clay soldiers buried with emperor
buried in a grave shaped like a cross

Page 73

Egypt
shenti
double crown
wax promade on wig
braided wig
red fingernails
red ankhs on palm
false beard
Greece
chiton
peplos
headband
Rome
toga virilis
false hair curls
white face powder
wedding band showing clasped hands
India
pigtails
sari
red dot on forehead
turban
cashmere
chintz
intricate henna hands/feet patterns
culottes
China
quilted jacket
cotton pants and shirt
paddy hat
silk dresses
long mustache